THINK o

THINK or Lose Everything

R. Carroll Gillham

Visit www.booksurge.com to order additional copies.

THINK or Lose Everything

CONTENTS

Chapter One   WHAT ABOUT BOB   1

Chapter Two   EDUCATION   7

Chapter Three   LEGAL SYSTEM AND POLITICS   15

Chapter Four   MEDIA AND ENTERTAINMENT   25

Chapter Five   RELIGION   35

Chapter Six   SPORTS AND AL'QUEDA   55

Chapter Seven   SEX   61

Chapter Eight   ILLEGAL DRUGS   69

Chapter Nine   ILLEGAL IMMIGRATION   77

Chapter Ten   WAR   87

Chapter Eleven   CHANGE   93

Chapter Twelve   ONE WORLD ECONOMY   97

Chapter Thirteen   UNITED WE STAND,
DIVIDED WE FALL...   103

INTRODUCTION

You might ask yourself, how does someone get the inspiration to write a book? I have often asked myself similar questions, such as: what got Tiger started on golf, why did Roger pick up his first tennis racquet, how did Elvis know he could sing, what made Jay Leno tell his first joke, and what possessed Oprah to get in front of her first TV camera?

None of these people can actually tell you precisely, but I'll bet each and every one of them did what Neil Diamond sang about in one of my favorite songs..."I Am." May I suggest you download or even go to the trouble of buying the record If you do, you will learn a great deal about the human spirit.

My situation is very simple...a thought jumped into my head and I sat down at the Dell Computer, that I had here-to-fore used to browse the Internet and watch the market value of my portfolio slowly and yet inextricably decline. (My favorite not-so-funny line was...how did the DOWN JONES INDUSTRIAL AVERAGE DO TODAY?) Once in front of the computer, I jotted a few notes as an outline, and then I began typing. It has taken more than five months to complete, but it has been five of the most fulfilling months in my entire life. It is, next to the creation, gestation, birth, and growth of my daughter into womanhood, the most fulfilling, creative experience I could ever have hoped to accomplish.

My hope is that you will enjoy my book so much that you, too, will become inspired to do something extraordinary and self-fulfilling. GOOD LUCK!

To Bill O'Reilly, Rush Limbaugh,
Glenn Beck, Sean Hannity, Dennis Miller
Mack, Helen and, of course
TARA ELIZABETH
They all gave me the inspiration, fire, and
belief in myself to create this work.

WHAT ABOUT BOB

I was born in Hobbs, New Mexico in 1942 to hard working parents. My father (Mack) was an oilfield mechanic and my mother (Helen) was a secretary. Our family moved a lot but ended up in Odessa, Texas...a town that was highly dependent on oil production.

Odessa later became famous as a football powerhouse in FRIDAY NIGHT LIGHTS...a largely nonfiction novel about my alma mater Permian High School also known as The Permian Panthers also known as the home of MOJO!—A fearsome juggernaut of high school football to be feared by all during the 1970's and 1980's. In fact, I was in the first graduation class of Permian and have proudly been memorialized by having my name etched into the marble base of THE PANTHER statue along with the names of the other initial graduates in 1960.

We moved to Odessa in 1946 and lived in a small, two-bedroom house until 1954. I began reading at an early age because there was no TV. In addition to reading everything I could get my hands on, I also listened to the family radio for hours and hours. The combination of reading and radio created an active and sometimes vivid imagination and the ability to THINK. Because TV had not reached Odessa, my brain was allowed, or rather forced, to use a much-maligned talent...that being THINKING for myself rather than being spoon fed by a hypnotic boob tube anchorman, talk show host, or some other molder of public opinion.

As a young man, I began my growth as an independent worker and thinker by securing my first job as a newspaper delivery boy at age 8. I not only got up at 4:30 a.m. and delivered my route but also delivered by hand to the local hospital before I had to get to school at 8 a.m. I was a fairly good student but had to study hard to make good grades. My parents were good parents, but didn't put a lot of pressure on us to excel. I pushed myself and became fairly self reliant in developing my own persona. One of the most important things that happened to me was an eye infection that kept me out of school for a few weeks. During that time, I found a huge book called THE VOLUME LIBRARY. It was at least 9 inches thick and crammed full of information and knowledge. I read this book cover to cover and it opened my mind to all things from A to Z from alpha to omega, from Christianity to Islam to Judaism to Buddhism to Hinduism, from Capitalism to Socialism to Communism. So much information was included succinctly, and it created in me the desire to know more so I became a voracious reader. All this gave me the ability to Think for myself based on my own evaluation of information.

I don't need Tom Brokow, Dan Rather, Douglas Edwards, Walter Cronkite and so on or a talk show host to tell me what the news means. I remember two anchormen on ABC on Channel 7 Eyewitness News when I lived in New York City from the late 1960's to the early 1980's (Roger Grimsby and Bill Buttel). To this day I still remember the sign on "...this is Roger Grimsby, Hear Now the News." It said it all...they presented the news as news, NOT their interpretation of the news and how we were supposed to understand the news rather than making up our own minds. After all, we have the God given ability to THINK and do not need to be directed by one of these gentlemen or ladies as to how we should interpret anything. Even as much as I enjoyed Jack Parr and Johnny Carson, these shows were almost exclusively entertainment oriented with little politically influential material. Their purpose was to entertain, NOT to sway and mold public opinion to their own persuasion. "Where have you gone Jolting Joe?" THINK!

After graduating from The University of Texas, Austin in 1970, I returned to New York City and began my career in finance. During my almost 20 years in New York, I had the pleasure of meeting and working with Arthur Levitt, David Rockefeller, Ed Koch, and even George Soros. All of the corporate executives were directed and driven toward financial success; however, when it came to Mr. Soros, it was an entirely different situation. His agenda always had overtones of "believe as I do or get out!" This included his political and religious views as well as his business beliefs. If people didn't buy in (both his own employees and others who attended the meetings) they were strangely missing from the next meeting. After expressing my ideas in reply to his direct question in one meeting regarding my personal political persuasion, I was never invited to another meeting. It was that occurrence that jump started my thinking that there was a move afoot from high levels in many different arenas designed to slowly and covertly sway our individual way of thinking to a more uniform thought process...that being THEIR WAY.

Why do these individuals, corporate executives, media giants and government officials, have such an agenda? Their agendas include taking God out of the areas of Education, Law, Politics, and all forms of Media...they will continue to allow God in the churches but He should tread carefully or they will throw Him out of the temples.. That question will be answered in the following pages. Please remember, these are MY THOUGHTS and I encourage you to THINK and come up with your own individual thoughts and conclusions...that is the reason I decided to write this book. I KNOW I am RIGHT but that is right for BOB. Think and make it right for YOU!

The most important areas that I will deal with in this book are as follows: Education, Legal System, Media (including radio, TV, print publications), Politics, Religion, and Sex. I'm also going to throw in a highly personalized tirade on "Illegal" Immigration including a snippet on Illegal Drugs just to make sure I've covered all major topics of the day (except abortion, stem cell conflict, prostitution, athletes foot and of course, THE HEARTBREAK OF PSORAISIS). Just to stir up things, expand the focus of the book, and, of course, to reach a large reading audience (REMEMBER...It's Not About The

Money) I decided to add a short chapter comparing SPORTS with AL'QUEDA and three even shorter chapters on, WAR, CHANGE, and ONE WORLD ECONOMY (that includes debunking the imminent threat of Global Warming).

Whether you agree with me or not is IRREVELANT... THE FACT THAT YOU BOUGHT THE BOOK means that you have taken the first step toward THINKING for yourself and that is what I hoped to achieve by writing this book. CONGRATULATIONS! Now before we begin, I want to give you some further insight into the author and some of the factors that developed my thought processes.

Again, I was born in a small town in New Mexico and raised in Odessa, Texas in a lower middleclass family. Everyone woke early at the same time and began the day ready for work. We kids made the beds, fed the animals, and got dressed for school. After returning from school, we were allowed to play or rest for an hour then we did our chores and finished our homework. Our homework was always checked by mom and/or dad. Then we all sat around reading or listening to the family radio waiting for dad to get home so we all could eat...there was NO snacking before dad arrived. After dinner, we sat around the living room and either talked about our day or read or listened to the radio...always together as a family. Occasionally when we had extra time on school nights, we went outside and played with our neighborhood friends. Every Sunday morning we dressed up and went to Sunday School then Church at THE FIRST METHODIST CHURCH. Our other religious education was Wednesday night prayer and family bible reading at home. During the summer we played ball, swam, and did chores, then it began all over again. I always earned my way and never received any financial help during my whole life. I saved my money and bought all of my cars with cash whenever I could afford it from the '51 Ford to my daughter's 2000 ML 320.

Now begin to Think and by Thinking for Yourself, you will save everything YOU hold dear, NOT WHAT OTHER PEOPLE ARE TRYING TO TELL YOU IS BEST FOR YOU AND IN YOUR BEST INTEREST. Please sit back in your favorite chair and read my creation...a creation that I never believed in my wildest dreams I would be capable of or able to write. Please let me know how you enjoyed my book. Personally, I have never enjoyed anything as much as sitting down in front of my Dell computer and letting my creativity flow. Sometimes I would get an inspiration during the day and if I was at work, I would scribble down the thought. At other times I would be asleep and wake up at 3 a.m., run to the computer and begin typing for 10 or 15 minutes or for hours. My greatest fear was (because I was almost totally computer illiterate and even relied on my seventeen-year-old daughter to log on) that after I had composed a brilliant paragraph or even chapter I would somehow erase everything. Luckily, she showed me the "save" function on Microsoft Word or we wouldn't be here right now... right? I truly look forward to your comments, thoughts and, of course, the expected criticism...Creative Criticism from the majority and Destructive Criticism from "those other guys."

EDUCATION

Basic to all peoples is gathering knowledge. By gathering knowledge, peoples improve their state, their self-esteem, and their abilities to live a productive life and lay the foundation for improved future generations.

America's educational system has always been, up until very recently, the fertile field for knowledge and ethical and personal development. As our public school system developed, it grew and evolved to fit the ever-changing nature of our nation and to become more aware of different nations and their unique systems and mores and values. This system was good enough to develop over 95% of our country's leaders, corporate executives, religious leaders, and, most importantly, all the rest of us.

When I was in public school in Odessa, the students were there to learn. We had no rights except to expect a good education. The students were students, teachers were teachers, and principals were principals. By and large, we accepted our roles and we respected and, yes, even sometimes feared the teachers and especially THE PRINCIPAL! Mr. McDonald and Mr. Langston dispensed justice evenly and with no explanation or political correctness. I know of no example where a student was reprimanded unjustly. In fact, the first time I ever saw any disobedience toward authority was in the 9th grade when a student actually attacked a teacher. The students were so upset that we quickly grabbed the student and took him to the principal's office. That student was never seen at school again and things went back to normal and we liked it that way. We were safe and secure in our capacity of students.

Of course, there were those incidents between students,

but we took care of those situations among ourselves. We didn't go home and whine to our parents or form gangs to solve our problems. And we never considered the need for an attorney or the "protection" of organizations such as our great protector... the ACLU. The leaders of our groups were the smart guys and girls or the jocks, but we didn't exist to downgrade or intimidate others...we just hung together and let the others do the same. We did, however, obey the rules while at school. Respect for authority and for our elders was always top-of-mind in all of us, not only because it was the right thing to do but also we knew that if our indiscretions made it home, we would suffer a worse result at the hands of our parents. In those days no one had heard of CPS...our parents took care of our discipline. I for one think that in over 90% of the cases of parental discipline, the punishment fits the situation. No, I'm not condoning child abuse (I've never struck my daughter and don't ever intend to), but I believe parents can do a far superior job disciplining their own children than some omnipotent governmental agency that, while having noble goals, should not impinge on day-to-day lives of American families.

I know one thing for sure; we NEVER HAD A COLUMBINE during the 1940's 1950's, 1960's, 1970's, 1980's or 1990's. This type of phenomenon did not begin to rear its ugly head until the 2000's. Why do you suppose this type of atrocity just surfaced within the last ten years? The answer is not poor potty training. Do you think it derives its genesis from poor parenting, television, rap music, the ACLU, permissive society, drugs, libertarian thinkers, and so on? If you focus on any one of these probable causes, you can develop a good case I'm sure. But the real reason is "all the above" and even more. We, the American people and parents, have become lazy and complacent and quite willing to shift the role model and authority figure from ourselves to anyone else. WE ARE THE CAUSE. But WE, THE AMERICAN PEOPLE, ARE ALSO THE ANSWER. Think!!

Once we entered high school, we became instantly smarter than every one...teachers, principals and parents. But because there was a system of "rules for all," our youthful attempts to overthrow the establishment were nipped in the bud and we soon became model students again...a role in which we felt more secure. We now made more and more serious mistakes as we spread our wings, but we always knew deep down that we had the system of teachers, principals, and parents there to provide us understanding even if it came with some well-deserved punishment. Punishment came in various forms ranging from swats to after school and Saturday study periods, but in no instance was the "punishment out of line for the crime." I was always the precocious child, the one who thought up things to do and allowed others to do it. When things went wrong, they got caught while angle-faced Robert was seldom rounded up for my fair share of the punishment.

There was never a reason for intervention by distraught parents or indignant parent groups or attorneys or even the ACLU...thank God there was no ACLU around then to "protect our rights." Therefore, we learned to make our own way within the System and grow as respectful individuals who could become self-reliant, productive members of the American society. We learned that for all actions there are reactions and consequences. We learned from our mistakes and errors, but I fear today no one is learning...they are being shielded from learning that life is full of opportunities and failures, happiness and sadness, joy and pain. Without these bumps in the road, how will our new generation learn to navigate their way through life? If the liberals have their way, there will always be THE GOVERNMENT to take care of us...personally I don't want a governmental father or mother and I believe NEITHER DO YOU! THINK!

Then for most of us came college. This new environment came as a growing experience with its own set of rules and its unique system. Of course, ours was very different because it was the time of "beatniks" and the Vietnam War. The vast majority of us set off on the task of learning the necessary skills to enter society and the business world after graduation. However, the War, "free love, peace and drugs," and political unrest created a subculture that would affect the very core of our country and its societal norms.

Flower Power and protests swept through the country and its entire education system. Most of us thought it was cute and a way to experiment with our newfound freedoms, but some took this to another level of political activism, violent protests, and serious drug and sex abuse. For those of us who had a solid foundation of religion and family values, we incorporated all these revolutionary ideas and actions and went on down the road, graduated, then either entered the armed forces or began our careers in the Brave New World. A much smaller group embraced this New World Order and either dropped out or began to actively attempt major changes to the American society and its political and religious foundations. For the most part, these individuals possessed fairly high I Q's and were from fairly affluent and/or liberal bent families. A few became anarchist and decided the only way to make change was violence; the others followed more conventional methods to achieve change.

The more violent individuals made some waves but by and large their efforts did not effect any systemic changes...they were a flash in the pan. The others entered society in many fields, but the really serious ones decided the best way to impact our society and effect the changes they wanted was to enter the various media fields. They entered radio, television, newspapers, and other print media as well as education, religion and the legal profession. These people were not in a big hurry...they witnessed the futile violent acts of their brothers that created a backlash in the American society that stifled their overt attempts to force change and decided to take a more covert approach. Slowly but surely, these people have been fairly successful infiltrating these essential areas of our society and planting their ideas, value systems, and liberal secular thought processes into our daily lives. By doing this slowly and insidiously, they hope to reshape our thought processes and values into an America that no longer has any Christian values, open and fair education system, fair and balanced media presentation, two party political system, and a legal system that (with all its flaws continues to be the best and fairest in the world) with the prodding of the ACLU no longer bears resemblance to what our Founding Fathers had in mind. In fact, I'm positive that if Thomas Jefferson and the "beltway boys" from that era would become violently ill if they were able to view our current state of legal and political affairs.

What better way to effect changes to an entire country's ideals, mores, ways of thinking, and overall value systems than to infiltrate the education system with the long term goal of slow but sure systemic change of the country's most valuable resources...its children and their minds. A great plan but they forgot one thing. The ability of the American people to discern right from wrong is very strong even with such a well thought out plan which is also well funded by those Soros types. Americans actually can think for themselves. Sometimes it takes a wakeup call to startle them to action. This book, I hope, will be one of the WAKEUP CALLS so we can once again throw the scoundrels out and get back to what America does best...being the shining light of freedom and hard work, creating capital, being the hope of the world, and fostering the belief that all men can reach for the stars.

Now let us look to the way all these "educational types" are able to effect changes to our system of education. Initially, as I explained earlier, they began infiltrating our schools and colleges and universities in the mid to late 1960's. Once in the system, they began to attempt to impose radical changes but for the most part they were unsuccessful. Even though most efforts failed, some took root and gave these "education terrorists" (ET's) hope that they would eventually be successful. They incorporated the old strategy of "yard by yard is very hard, but inch by inch it is a chinch!"

Once the first wave of these ET's had successfully entered the system...much like when a malignant organism enters the human body...they began incorporating their ideas and dogma into everyday classes for the students and into the teacher associations. Remember "inch by inch!" The most vile and insidious way to overthrow a family, city, state, or nation is by corrupting the minds of the children because if you are able to effect structural changes in the minds and spirits of the future generations, it won't take more than three or four generations to completely overthrow the original system. THINK!

To further solidify their positions, the next thing was to slowly but surely incorporate their thinking into the rest of the teachers and professors. What a fertile field for these caring "forward thinkers" is the pocket book of our admittedly under paid and under appreciated teaching staff. What better way is there to grow your legions than to be on the side of those you are trying to influence? The first thing is to infiltrate teacher unions...not that any union is bad, but for a thinker like me a union in the school is contrary to everything a free society wants. The next thing is to provide "TENURE" for these teachers. Do you actually understand what tenure is, or does, or causes to happen? THINK! Tenure assures incompetence. It is a program developed by the ET's to make sure that once they were in a position of power, they would NEVER have to relinquish that power.

Tenure is defined as "status afforded an employee indicating that the position or employment is permanent." Imagine what that kind of guarantee would do to your employment drive and motivation! Of course, on the surface this sounds like what all of us would want, BUT this is a guaranteed formula for mediocrity at best and failure at the worst. Do you want to be mediocre? Do you want to be a failure? I'm sure that every day of your life you have awakened, jumped out of bed, looked in the mirror and said "Here is another day for me to prove my mediocrity," (or even better)..."Here is another day for me to fail again." This' is NOT THE AMERICAN WAY!...It is socialism at its best and WE will not accept these ET's solution to improve our way of life. THINK!

Just think, do you want a tenured, lazy, slovenly, non-driven, underachiever to mold your children's minds? Of course not, but that is what is happening in today's halls of learning and enlightenment from kindergarten all the way up to Harvard and Yale and yes even Slippery Rock University. Tenure is everywhere in academia. It must be eradicated and we must bring back the old American ethic of constant hard work in order to gain self-pride and achieve a better lifestyle for yourself and your family. The way to earn more money is to work harder and smarter. Please understand, I am on the teacher's and professor's side. I do not agree with arbitrary dismissal of any employee in any field of work, BUT I do not believe in "no cut contracts"...they are the pathway to mediocrity at best and abject failure at the other end of the spectrum. THINK!

Some of the most intelligent and dedicated and caring people I have ever known have been in the education system. These are inspired people who dearly love their jobs and the children to whom they minister. I truly believe teachers are, without question, God's gift to all civilizations. Why then am I attacking bastions of the system...those being tenure and teacher unions?

First of all, let me state that I am not attacking you teachers personally or the intrinsic nature of your noble profession. I am attacking the unions because unions are antiquated, ineffectual and, in today's world, on the road to extinction because, just like the dinosaurs, if you do not adapt and evolve you are doomed. Now here come all the union members and their hierarchy ready to lynch me or brand me a union hater. Not so, unions have been a progressive, inventive, and valuable force in America's labor movement for well over two hundred years. The point I'm trying to make is...no matter how worthy labor unions have been in the history of America...they must adapt to the ever changing labor situation in our country. I'm trying to awaken these dinosaurs to the truth of today's developing labor Darwinism...to graduate from their paradigm of hundreds of years of complacency. If they are unable or unwilling to effect changes in their unions' systems, the entire union concept will vanish as surely as the Tyrannosaurus Rex. THINK!

Why should our nation's most valuable resource...that being THE TEACHERS OF OUR CHILDREN...sit near the bottom of the salary totem pole? What is our value system? When we pay millions of dollars to sports figures, sometimes even HUNDREDS OF MILLIONS OF DOLLARS to punt, pass, or kick a ball, throw, hit or catch a ball, shoot, block or dunk a ball, race a souped-up car around a track in a continuous left turn, and so on, how can we look at ourselves and say that thirty, forty, fifty, and yes even a hundred thousand dollars per annum is out of line for a teacher and molder of our country's future work force be they laborers, doctors, lawyers, IT pros, or yes even politicians? Surely we as ordinary citizens, without the slow but sure, inch by inch manipulation of these maggots, would NEVER have accepted a $250,000,000 contract for a 31 year old soccer player or a $200,000,000 contract for a baseball pitcher who has NEVER played in The American or National Leagues. Ask yourself...if we took ourselves back to even 1990... wouldn't you have gone crazy if you had turned on the radio or TV and heard the sports commentator report that a sports figure was getting a contract to play a "child's" game worth 40 or 50 times what the President of the United States makes! Yes, if you go inch by inch, it IS a cinch! THINK!

Our teachers need MORE...More RESPECT, More RESPONSIBILITY, More AUTHORITY, and yes even More MONEY$$$$$$$$$$$$...Don't YOU AGREE????? If you do not agree, it leads me to one of two assumptions. One, you are one of THEM and therefore I don't GIVE A DAMN about what you think because you don't think...you are ruled by personal emotion, not what's in the best interest of America...And to these types I say "get with the program or GET OUT!" My second assumption (and yes I am aware that when you assume you make an ass out of you and me) is that you must be one of these mindless individuals who is content to be brainwashed by these Soros types and sit mesmerized in front of your TV or reading your Old York Times and happily turn into the Couch Potato they want you to be. You are the fodder they feed on... breakfast, lunch and dinner. There must be some desire in you to change; otherwise you would not have bought this book, much less made it this far into my novel. THINK!

LEGAL SYSTEM AND POLITICS

Rather than opening up myself to enormous criticism from both liberals and conservatives, I will state again, these are my own thoughts and I hope both sides have a field day condemning my points of view because in doing so...they are THINKING and that is the purpose of this book. I have decided to combine the two subjects of the legal system and politics because they are so inextricably intertwined.

The founding fathers had enormous pressures on them because they were drafting documents that would become the framework of their new country. When they authored the Constitution, they purposely kept it short and open to interpretation. Were they stupid or just very hopeful that this country would endure and use this basic document as a living template allowing for necessary evolutionary changes? Based on their rather narrow focus in the 1780's, these people were brilliant in designing America's basic legal documents to hold true and yet be flexible enough to endure for needs in the 2000's.

Take a fair look back into what the United States were in the 1780's. There was a loose knit union of 13 states none of which were any more advanced in their political expertise than a human being is in the first month of gestation. These men, none of whom had ever authored nation forming documents, talked, discussed, compromised, and thought for months and months before completing The Declaration of Independence and the Constitution. They realized full well that theirs was an ominous task but one that had to be accomplished in short order to prevent petty bickering, second guessing and, of course, the ever present need to place personal preferences and priorities over the needs of this new fledgling country. To their credit the United States stands today, approximately 250 years later, as the most prominent and quintessential embodiment of Democracy in the history of the world. Good show guys...we couldn't have done it without you! But fear not; some of our "finest" are trying their best to not only fine tune your fabulous documents with their liberal secular slant on what they believe you guys actually meant but to grossly adapt your works into something akin to a <u>Readers' Digest</u> version of <u>War and Peace</u> or <u>The Bible</u> or <u>The Torah</u> or <u>The Koran</u>. As my father once told me..."there are some people who can screw up a steel ball with a rubber hammer." My father died in 1973 but must have foreseen the ACLU and all the other "protectors of every one's rights without considering the obvious fact that with rights also come RESPONSIBILITIES. Any fool can throw stones but it takes real intelligence, empathy, and the human traits of love and understanding to build something that will endure and be a nurturing environment to its citizenry.

Contrary to what the rich, disassociated, liberal-minded Ted Kennedy types think, WE THE PEOPLE are not interested in the government taking care of us morally, spiritually, religiously, or financially. Of course, there are those who have "bought in" and are willing generation after generation to humble themselves before the almighty Federal Government. But WE THE PEOPLE are a proud, hard working group who want and NEED to take care of ourselves and our families with only the minimum of required governmental direction. Hey Ted, who the hell are you to presuppose that your pampered, protected, elitist background gives you the right—much less the insight—into how the "average" US citizens think or what they need from "big brother" government? You who never held a real job but rather were given everything from the Kennedy Trust Funds; you who never got your nails dirty except maybe when you climbed out of the muddy banks of Chappaquiddick River, or you who would have been just another bumbling rich guy if your brothers had not had their successes, have no right or insight in to effecting laws that will impact OUR lives. Get out Ted; everyone knows you are a joke.

Any country needs some form of appointed or elected leadership in order to have a national presence in the world and carry out the will of its citizenry. That leadership governs at the will of the people and carries out the established laws, and only when it becomes the people's wishes should any laws be amended or eliminated or new laws created. We do not need any of "the liberal boys and girls" to tell us what our forefathers meant by "is." We all know that is...is, and is not...is not! We actually only need our federal, state, and local leaders to honor and enforce the laws of the land and provide safety for us against all of our country's enemies. We ARE NOT interested in anyone's need for "political correctness." And while we are on the subject of what we do not need...we DO NOT NEED ANY ONE from George Soros to Alec Baldwin to The Dixie Chicks, to various media moguls to do anything except do what they do best. George should make money in the U. S. send it to the Netherlands Antilles and pay no taxes; Alex should keep acting outside the U. S. as he promised when George W. was elected... were you just acting or are you just another big mouthed liberal liar; Chicks keep singing on key and leave your comments where they belong...on the cutting room floor; and you media types KEEP TO REPORTING THE NEWS not slanting or spinning news. News is news is news...NOT what you choose to report or your interpretation of what has happened. Go back to presenting news...that is your job. You guys are not elected by the people; therefore, you have no popular mandate to do anything except report the news as it occurs. You all might think your position empowers you to have more power than you do... but you do not. We actually do not care what YOU think; you do but you are in the minority! We will get back to these guys later in the book. REMEMBER you are REPORTERS. If you have lost sight of what a reporter does...I will remind you...a reporter is a person who gives a detailed account of an event, situation, and so on based on observation or inquiry. If you guys want to uncloak yourselves from the protection afforded by freedom of the press, then stop calling yourselves reporters and call yourselves what you have become...NEWS LOBBYISTS.

Now back to the legal system...actually the system is fine but it is not well. The system has become ill because of a few things that can and should be rectified in short order. The two main things that adversely impact our legal system are Lobbyists and the lack of Term Limits. Both of these foster an aura of GREED in our lawmakers. And to amend a quote from one of Michael Douglas' films..."greed for the lack of a different word is (NOT) good." We MUST become aware that our current lawmakers are being seduced by the age old, Good-old-Boy network that only insures one thing and that one thing IS NOT what is best for the people who elected them. After getting elected based on their noble ideals that they espoused while on the election trail, they get to Washington and promptly get sucked into the Black Hole of greed and...what will it take for me to get reelected. I would venture to guess that our Senate and House members spend less than 20% of their terms doing good for the people and protecting the rights, property, and lives of their constituents. Party, Party, Party; Lie, Lie, Lie; Gifts, Gifts, Gifts: Trips, Trips, Trips; Compromise, Compromise, Compromise; Fit in, Fit in, Fit in;...give up your individual pride and honor in order to get reelected. The other 80% of their time is dedicated to finding ways to ensure that they will get re-elected. You might ask yourself...why do these people want this job that only pays $200,000 per year when most of them make far more than that amount in their present situation? And why did they spend Millions and Millions to get this position? WHY, WHY, WHY?

We must design some form of term limits in order to get rid of the Ted Kennedy types who only exist to foster their own agendas. Truly no one actually believes that Ted cares about anyone other than Ted. Some say he is a great leader, but they are only sucking up to him because of his Good-old-Boy power base that he has gained over the last 40 years. Throw him out with all the Good old Boys whether they are Republican or Democrat. We need a group of freshly scrubbed new electorate that owe allegiance only to the people who elected them to honorably uphold the laws of this country and to do their best to make our country a better place for us and our children. THINK!

WE MUST GET RID OF ALL LOBBYSTS...they serve no good purpose. There are better ways of getting your ideas and needs in front of your congressmen than to have a bunch of malignant influence peddlers corrupting our elected officials by dangling money, drugs, prostitutes, and the hope for longer terms assistance...IF ONLY YOU'LL VOTE FOR MY PEOPLE'S BILLS. This is corruption at its finest. Who the hell ever gave these maggots the right to exist or did they just show up one day and set up shop with a bag of money? They are the "rotten apple" in the barrel and must be thrown out before we can move forward to the noble ideals and direction of our forefathers.

Corruption, power brokerage, and far left liberal influence also spreads their ugly heads into our legal system. There are many areas within the legal system so I will focus on a scant few but needless to say I could write a second or even third book on what is not covered in this book (smells like a sequel, doesn't it?). The areas that I want to focus on are the judiciary and the parole systems because these two areas are so influential in our day- to-day lives and have enormous impact on society.

What a horrific feeling it must be to any parent to have something unspeakable done to their innocent children...then have the perpetrator apprehended...then after months of legal wrangling (probably with the "alleged" perpetrator out on bond because no one wants to impinge upon his/her civil rights) have a trial and have the judge sentence this Devilish person to be freed on a technicality or sentenced to anything less than life in prison or death! If you don't agree, that is your right in America, BUT if you have any other opinion, I can only say...you are totally amoral; shame on you! What more despicable act can be taken than inflicting fear, pain, and immoral acts upon a defenseless, innocent, trusting child. Further, once the child has been harmed, that child will never be the same again, and it is highly likely that that child will grow up to abuse other people in much the same manner, but never-the-less the beauty of that child will be forever tarnished.

During these trials, if there is one, our system requires this traumatized child to appear in court, face the attacker, and suffer the badgering of the defense attorney because our system of justice has not moved in the 21st century. Most applicable laws were incorporated into our legal system in the 19th and early 20th centuries when crimes like these weren't as numerous and there was not any American Criminal Liberties Union or liberally bent, sectarian secular judges waving their gavels over the courts of the US. Judges are not empowered to interpret the laws. Their duty is to preside over courts of law, make sure all involved abide by the law, and dispense justice in accordance to established law. ONLY THIS AND NOTHING MORE! But in today's world, these justices have become emboldened with the encouragement of well-financed secularists (hello George) hell bent on making everything legal or searching for reasons behind this "unfortunate situation." I personally DO NOT BELIEVE or GIVE ANY CREEDANCE to the "bad potty training" excuse or the newest ones..."I only did this because the other children didn't like me and made fun of me," or "I was High and didn't know what I was doing." These and all the other lame excuses are only that...excuses and NOT GET OUT OF JAIL reasons!

We all make mistakes but we can't just say I'm sorry, I did that because...and the reason that we can't do this is the fact that we have a codified set of laws that MUST be adhered to or these laws might as well be shredded. Isn't that a coincidence? That is exactly what the Soros types (let's start calling them ST's because I'm tired of giving him credit) want...to make everything legal. Their philosophy is that if there are no laws...there is no crime. Without crime we need no police, no police cars burning up gas, no need for police stations or courthouses, no stenographers, no bailiffs, no gavels, no jails, no parole officers, no ankle bracelets, no syringes and needles, and so on. Look at all we are saving! Only one small problem...all the bad guys are roaming our streets and neighborhoods robbing, stealing, raping, beating, killing, burning, and other things. Now isn't that a sight that makes you want to go out and elect Senators, Representatives, and even Presidents that are ST's? Before we inch-by-inch ourselves into accepting the no crime era, we have the judiciary stoking the secular engines by interpreting existing laws—not enforcing them.

While the judges have been ajudging, the parole officers have been aparoling. (Bad language but I thought you might enjoy a little diversion at this point in the book.) I believe these people actually try to do a decent job, BUT I do not understand granting time off for good behavior to pedophiles, rapists, drug dealers, or murderers among many others too numerous to mention. No "good behavior" in a prison is good enough to warrant release of anyone who has harmed a child or inflicted himself upon a woman or become the cause of another person's addiction or taken someone's life. My belief is that, if these people are released before their sentence has been served, and if that person commits another crime during his or her parole, the parole panel members should serve concurrent time in jail with the offender. This might sound severe; HOWEVER, I believe a crime is a crime and a sentence is a sentence and "that's all I've got to say about that!"

Let us now focus on a very specific situation. If a person is charged with DUI/DWI, he, as is his right, should be represented by an attorney. If that person has enough financial strength, he will probably get off with only a slap on the wrist or a very short sentence especially if it is a first time offense. That may be well and good because it is, after all, the American system of justice. However, now that this person "gets away with it," he sees that he has done nothing wrong and goes out and does it again and again until some innocent person or family gets killed by this person who is so stupid that he doesn't think about what his irresponsible actions could inflict on others. We need to be accountable for our actions every time. Accountability is what happens to us if we break the rules of society...this is the converse of civil rights...it is CIVIL RESPONSIBILITY! I could go on and on about up and down, left and right, debits and credits, right and wrong, life and death, and so on but you get the idea.

If we all understand this simple concept, why then are the Kennedys, Lays, Stewarts, popular actors and actresses, sports figures, and others afforded special treatment by our law enforcement agencies and legal system. They already have been blessed by God with money, prestige, and power...why do they expect and yes, DEMAND, better, more favorable treatment when they have committed the same offense as a day laborer? WHY? WHY? WHY? These people and their attorneys do not have one honest (full disclosure) answer to this question. The answer we are always given and the one we have all been brainwashed into believing is either "they have better attorneys" or "because of their status, they deserve more leniency and understanding than the rest of us because of their importance to the community." HOW STUPID DO THESE PEOPLE THINK WE ARE? And how long do they expect to continue this charade? Let's end this NOW! If indeed we were all "created equal"...what went wrong? THINK!!!!THINK!!!!

You cannot imagine how much better our world would be if, "not only we were all created equal" BUT "we were also treated equally!" Be honest with yourself; do you really believe that a Ted Kennedy type deserves even one iota more (or less) consideration than does your next-door neighbor or the guy who picks up your garbage? THINK!!! Don't buy into their crap. THINK!!!!THINK!!!!THINK!!!!

Now that we have those issues exposed to the pure light of you the American people, I am sure that you will now begin to rally around the rights of (NOT THE CRIMINALS) the rest of us who follow the rules of society. IT IS NOT WRONG OR UNCHRISTIAN TO DEMAND JUSTICE FOR ALL THOSE CONVICTED OF ALL

CRIMES. Stop letting the liberal, leftist, lunatic fringe (the tail) wag the other 99% of the other law-abiding citizens (the dog). You have rights, too, and your rights should and MUST supercede the criminal's rights. After all, he gave up his civil rights when he decided to take yours...DIDN'T HE?

But you must become more vocal than the criminals and their loudmouthed advocates and stop allowing these aggressive libertarians to reshape this wonderful country's legal system... do it now, do it today!

If that is not enough of a rah-rah for you to get you up off your complacent rear end...I have a few adrenaline inducing examples of why you should take action NOW!

I will end this section with one more example of how we have been duped into believing that we (primarily Christians) MUST show mercy to everyone. WRONG!!!!!

For example, those individuals who choose to break the laws of our country, even for the first time and are incarcerated, should lose all their civil rights because their actions have impinged upon someone else's civil rights. Because they choose to act in this manner, while they are incarcerated, they should be confined to a cell 24/7 until they are released. Think that is cruel and unusual punishment? Do you think that these criminals deserve television privileges? Do you believe they deserve free time to walk around the yard? Do you believe they deserve special meals? Do you believe they deserve communication privileges with their families? Do you believe they deserve connubial visits with their significant others? To people like you, I say you are 100% completely, absolutely WRONG! If you feel so strongly that you disagree, I will make myself available in a neutral forum to debate this problem. Well, what would you feel (Mr. Kennedy), if a person acted directly against you and your family? Would you be as magnanimous and forgiving as you appear to be when these crimes are directed to people other than the elite Kennedy clan? I know that would be hard to do since you live in a secluded, fenced, guarded compound. Oh, by the way, why do you feel the need of fences and guards?...possibly because you think your life and property is more valuable than the rest of ours because you inherited so much money and you feel superior! YOU ARE WRONG MR. KENNEDY. Come on down and live with us for one month (say work on a sanitation truck for one day, the MTA for 4 days, a fishing boat for a week, and enjoy the rest of your month working in a prison). DEAL

OR NO DEAL? Probably you are too busy trying to intimidate your colleagues into passing laws to benefit the needy and the ordinary people. Question readers...do you feel that you are ORDINARY? Please remember, these types always are trying to hoodwink you into believing that they care. THEY DO NOT!!!!!! What they are trying to achieve is garnering a few more votes to ensure that they can remain in office one more term.

The ST's haven't achieved their End Game yet, but they are working diligently and are emboldened and encouraged by their successes to date. Be more diligent, be proud, and above all beware of all those guys who have your best interest at heart but have never met you! THINK!

MEDIA AND ENTERTAINMENT

Where to start on media? You have so many areas that daily...yes even hourly...bombard us all with differing degrees of deceit or deception all in the name of news or entertainment. The areas of radio, TV, newspapers, magazines, periodicals, books, movies, and now the Internet are the perfect salesmen for slanting news or ideas to the wishes of the "masters of spin."

As early as medieval times, some people realized that the way to gain power was not by the sword but rather the pen. Some of the most powerful leaders of the world utilized the then most popular media to mold popular opinion for their own ends. Some notable examples were Hitler, Emperor Hiriohito, Stalin, Chairman Mao Ze Dong and now Osama Ben Laden and don't forget William J. Clinton (the man who the media believed could do nothing wrong even when he was caught with his pants down). In fact, Mr. Clinton took it another step by making us all try to understand the meaning of "is." If the spin-doctors can make us question the meaning of a two-letter word, just think what they can do with a three-letter word...for instance "sex." Then take it another step to what they can do with sentences, paragraphs, and so on all the way up to concepts and ideas and even beliefs!

Now let's take this media coercive plan into various areas of our daily lives. You might not even notice the slow but sure insidious nature of this plan because any slow acting plan is accepted and assimilated, until it becomes the norm. Remember, the old adage "yard by yard is very hard but inch by inch is a cinch." And don't forget the old truism..."a lie told a thousand times becomes the truth!" I, like you, lived my life as a normal

American...I woke up, went to work, came home to my family, ate, and sat down to watch TV or listen to the radio or read a book. Day by day we have all been indoctrinated with slightly different thought patterns bombarding us from all segments of media and entertainment without us being even slightly aware...it is a slow, insidious form of "brainwashing." I know, now you're saying, "Here's another nut waving the American flag and shouting here comes the enemies of America." But just reflect back even a few years and try to remember how we evolved from the insinuated murder or rape scene in the 1960's and 1970's and even the 1980's to graphic scenes of gang rapes and brutal dismembering murders. And don't forget the evolution of the music industry from "Peggy Sue" to today's "Let's Kill the Bitch." These media moles (MMs) are people who began burying themselves in radio, TV, music, movies, newspapers, and other print media in the 1960's and 1970's. Once buried, they began implementation of their plan to desensitize the American psyche to debauchery in every form including everything from child abuse to bestiality all the way to "snuff films!" The print MMs were just as active by bringing in more and more licentious articles in a deliberate plan to make these actions more palatable to the American public. Just think, would you in your wildest dreams have imagined opening your newspaper or favorite magazine in 1980, 1990, or even 2005 to see a popular singing star's crotch or reading graphic stories depicting abhorrent situations? NO, YOU WOULD NOT HAVE!!! But it has now become as ingrained in our culture as blue berry pie. And they are not done yet. THINK!!

Sports stars (who used to be our idols and role models) now routinely jump into the stands and assault the fans or assault each other or even the coaches and referees. Now this action is occurring within the sporting arenas, but what about their off court or off field antics? These over paid thugs and hoodlums don't even consider, if they rape someone, shoot at anyone, or skip out on bills they owe, that they should be held accountable. But what should we expect? After all we were the ones who sat back and allowed these athletes (much like we have rap singers) to shove their success in everyone's face and say..."I don't give a damn about what you think...my name is KobLtrlLudiFitiPak and the law don't get in my grill because I B Superman and your laws don't apply to me." THINK!!!

Personally, I have never been a firebrand for either the conservative or the liberal side. Rather I, like you, have been a dutiful American believing in "truth, justice and the American way." I read the newspapers, read my share of books, listened to the radio, watched TV, and sat back and accepted my share of The American Way of Life. Some of my favorite entertainers are Alec Baldwin, Robert Redford, Barbara Streisand, Susan Sarandon, Dustin Hoffman, and George Clooney among many others too numerous to list. I have enjoyed their movies and songs for years and always held them to a high degree of reverence because they are "stars." Because of their star status, they have been allowed by all of us to freely express their own opinions (without question), and they have abused our trust and their status to promote their own political and social agendas. After listening to these entertainer types espouse all that is negative with our country without divulging to us their plan to improve it AND with none of them having a degree in political science or law, I have come to the conclusion that these types (after living in a true make believe world their entire lives) are only trying to stay in the limelight in the only way they know... that being opening their mouths and following a script that has no repercussions. I wonder what type of life these "stars" would be enjoying if they were born and raised in Mexico? Of course, in their fantasy world the songs end and another one starts with no repercussions, no loss of life or freedom, or at the end of the movie, it's over and a new movie is right around the corner... again, nothing disastrous, just another day in Hollywood. Why do we place any credence in their opinions? The answer my friend is blowing in the wind...we should listen to their rhetoric and give it its due consideration and NOTHING MORE. After all, these are entertainers ,NOT statesmen, but Thank God we live in America where all people are allowed to express their opinions.

The movie and other entertainment media types including TV have been very busy bees with their slow but sure incursions into the moral fabric and belief systems of America. Later on, I will get into the slow but sure (inch by inch) method of spreading their malignant ideas into the minds and moral fiber of the country.

Today, no one even gasps at the F-word or viewing gang rapes of underage children, or documentaries extolling the virtues of pedophilia, blowing up government buildings, or even depicting the assassination of our current President, George W. Bush. When I was a child and even when I was a teenager, movies and entertainment media was just that...ENTERTAINMENT. However, along came the media terrorists (MT's) with slow but sure introduction of what had here-to-fore been classified as pornography, heresy, disgusting, or just bad taste. To our discredit WE the consuming public (with intense promoting by the MT'S using every media source) bit hook-line-and sinker and voted with our hard earned dollars. To again use one of the most stupid lines ever..."It's not the money," but it is the money because had we not voted with our dollars, these types would not have gotten so powerful and brazen as they are today. Shame on us! THINK!

All the same can be said for the print media, especially major newspapers such as The Washington Post and The New York Times. If you have ever had the opportunity to read The Times as I did when I lived in New York City for over a decade, then you will know that, if operated correctly, The Times can once again become a great newspaper. I actually enjoyed the paper because it had so many sections that informed me about sports, plays, music, theater, and other events. However, after I had finished those sections I threw the rest into the trash because it never provided any other point of view that did not have a liberal bent. The paper was so obviously biased that you could not even find a contrary opinion in the editorial section. If you have the displeasure to read The New York Times now (20 years later), you will find the worst form of biased depiction of the news. The whole newspaper organization from its ownership to the newest contributor would be welcomed with open arms in any propaganda mill thought up by Nazi Germany, Communist China, or Radio Free Al' Queda.

When I was a child, my first job was delivering newspapers. I delivered the Odessa American, The Fort Worth Star Telegram and even a unique paper called GRIT. At the Odessa paper, I was able to see the entire operation from the reporters to the press operators. I enjoyed working with these people and even got to go out on a few stories and sat there as the reporters typed their stories. It was very exciting to me to read the stories when I got home and know I had lived through the entire story. This was back in the early 1950's and all the paper did was report the news. What a refreshing concept that evidently is completely lost in today's Times where all they have is "all the news fit to slant." The trouble is that it is not just the Times...it is a good estimate that well over 80% of the major media sources are one sided spinners. With a daily, and yes even hourly, dose of one-sided "slanted news," even the most astute consumer would eventually be converted to the liberal point of view. This is a perfect example of...a lie told a thousand times becomes the truth. PLEASE BE AWARE...PLEASE THINK FOR YOURSELF!

Now you might ask yourself...why are these media sources so overwhelmingly left wing liberal in their presentation of the news or entertainment? And, when questioned, they always cloak themselves in the robes of The First Amendment or, if that fails, they claim creative license or, if these fail, they fall back on "we are only providing what the American people want." They may be right on any or all these arguments BUT the real reason behind this leftward leaning is the Soros types' maniacal obsession with taking we out of We The People and GOD out of IN GOD WE TRUST. Oops, there is that nasty WE again. The point that you might find interesting is that the majority of these liberal thinkers were born to wealth and have never worked for hourly wages, but they are sure they know what is good and right for the "average American" and, of course, they also know what all the minorities and poor desire. What insight

from demigods most of who have NEVER gone a day without
food, had to decide between Wal-Mart or the Salvation Army,
had to turn off the air conditioner to save money on a 100 degree
day, or worn clothes/shoes six months after they ceased to be
comfortable. These guys have to decide between Filet Mignon
and Lobster, Sax or Bergdorf's, the temperature is controlled
by someone else...or better be, and their clothing is always of
impeccable taste.

THINK...what does it take for these liberals to be able to
sit on high and pronounce what is good for the rest of us mere
mortals? YES you are right!!! MONEY!

But if you look carefully, it is not THE MONEY, but
if not the money then what? We ordinary people have a hard
time understanding what could be more important than money
primarily because we spend most of our lives trying to make
just enough money to have a fairly comfortable existence. So
to us having a lot of money equates to having a lot of security
and comfort and fun. We have no point of reference to indicate
otherwise. But to these privileged, liberal leftists the END
GAME is POWER! They have nothing else to do all day but
figure out how to stir things up because they are BORED.

These people have no challenges left in their world...they
have all the money they could never spend; all the best food; all
the best clothing; all the most expensive cars, boats and planes;
all, all, all. Believe it or not fellow Americans, these people are
BORED, BORED, BORED. What is left for people in this
horrible situation? They decide to tinker with the status quo,
stir up things in order to make things more exciting for them
and further expand the power they have. Just think how much
devilment you and I could get into if we had everything and too
much time to fill. THINK! This is actually what you can now
understand is the motive behind their (to us) insanity.

Now that you understand the real reason these types do
what they do, you don't have to sit back, scratch your head
and say...Why do these idiots do what they do or think the
way they think? You have the ability to think for yourself so
just sit back alone or with your loved one(s) and have a family

discussion...YES a discussion which implies that you talk and listen using you own God Given mouth, ears, and brain AND without the TV or Radio blaring out their incessant, slanted views on everything from The War in Iraq to the abducted child somewhere in the US or the almost daily tirades between Rosie and The Donald. You will find it very stimulating conversing with your spouse, children, friends, and others whose ideas mean a lot more to you than most of the news slant clowns on the public wave links. Now please remember Rome wasn't built in a day and therefore your communication skills are probably a little rusty AND you might find out that your significant others may not feel exactly like you do. In fact, I will be willing to guess that you will be absolutely astounded by their ideas and how they differ from yours...especially your children's ideas. Face it; we are in an ever and rapidly changing society and world so grab hold or get left behind. I for one am 64 and the only reason I haven't given up and toddled off to the farm is that I am blessed with a seventeen-year-old daughter. She keeps me on my toes and up to date and constantly challenged and amazed with how they see my world. We no longer live in an 8-track world and somehow I missed the cassette age and went directly to CD's and DVD's (which I was pleased to learn has nothing to do with STD's).

Now remember, I broached the subject of inch by inch... the next very small but effective approach used by our Media Maggots is the "but or however" ploy. I love you BUT; I agree with you wholeheartedly HOWEVER. You see how this is going, yes? Yes you do NOW, BUT, BUT, BUT. This is exactly what I am talking about. Why can't these people just open their mouths or pens and make a simple statement as a yes or a no? The answer my friend (as one of my adolescent idols said in song) is blowing in the wind. We must not let this winds of change change us just to effect a change. Confusing? Probably, but let me continue. Change just for change's sake is full of uncertainty. There must be a positive reason to change with a hopefully better result than is possible with the current situation. As the in-crowd would say...THE END GAME...(which I presume to mean the outcome) is the newest catch phrase. Hope I got that right.

To say the least, the abilities of these media spinners are almost limitless. They have all the time in the world to sit around and develop (not report) their views as to how they are going to report what the story really means. They have almost endless funding from the Soros types. They have a virtual monopoly. And if that is not enough, they have as the ace-in-the-hole The FIRST AMENDMENT! Circle the wagons boys...we can say, do or imply almost anything with impunity, insinuate, cast doubt, allege, make statements, express conjecture, or JUST MAKE UP STORIES. No one can mess with us because we have FREEDOM OF THE PRESS...don't even try or we'll have our constitutional mad dog attorneys and the American Criminal Liberty Union on you like a duck on a June bug. We got everyone so messed up they don't even know if is is or what sex is...We got the American public right where we want them and we've messed up their thought and values system so much they are impotent. WRONG! We might have become a little lazy and lackadaisical for a while, but George you and the Boys and Girls better watch out because things are about to change. Remember, you can only go so far left then there is no room LEFT and then you fall off the table! So long George, you've fired your best shots and there is not enough Viagra left for you to get up for another round. With any luck, you'll find a nice retirement in the Netherlands Antilles near all your money that you failed to pay taxes on.

As a parting shot on the MT's, I want you to remember an old adage taught to us early in life..."statistics don't lie"... WRONG, WRONG, WRONG! In order to illustrate the fallacy of this adage AND the reason you should NEVER take any statistical evidence proffered by any of the MT's, I offer the following example: Sometime in the mid-1960's when we were in the middle of the Cold War, the United States agreed to send some of its premier athletes to Russia to compete with athletes from several countries including Russia's finest. This event was designed to help melt the Cold War through athletic competition. The events went off with great success and received constructive worldwide media coverage; however, one event didn't fare so well. All of the contestants in one long distance event failed to show with the exception of the Russian and the American. Rather than canceling the race, it was decided to have these two athletes compete one on one. The race was run and the American won...The headline in the Russian newspaper read...Russian athlete comes in second— American finishes next to last! Just imagine what The Old York Times could do with this event if they put their maniacal minds in high gear! THINK!

RELIGION

Now here we go...getting into a subject where only a fool would tread. I may be naming myself but this section will not get into which religion is right and which religion is wrong because I believe all religions are good and necessary for all humanity. Personally, I have never met a single individual who had a spirit strong enough or will strong enough to get them through life's trials and tribulations without at least once asking for help from some form of higher power or even a deity. I will (I hope) treat this subject with the reverence it deserves.

My own feelings are that if you have some belief that gives you solace in time of need or hope in time of despair or confidence when you are impotent or that inexplicable feeling of rapture when you begin having doubts of your immortality...you are on the right track no matter if you are Catholic, Protestant, Lutheran, Episcopalian, Buddhist, Hindi, Islamic, or whatever. Hope I didn't leave out too many of the great religions of the world. And, of course, I do not want to leave out the atheist religion (yes religion)...all those who express their total disbelief in a non-tangible higher power (deity), BUT they have a belief in their non-belief AND I am as certain as I am writing this book that when their own mortality is staring them in the face, these atheists will be the first to fall on their knees and ask for some form of Godly intervention on their behalf. So sit back and watch as these individuals who, for what ever reason, must raise their voices in denial to God, one by one find some personal reason to accept what the rest of us already know.

Why do we have or need religion? Who is God? Now these are two fairly difficult questions for a little guy from Odessa,

Texas, but here we go with my best thoughts drawing from my God given abilities, a good educational background, a lot of ups and downs…and some of those downs were deep knee bending downs, and general life experience over 64 odd years.

Let's jump right into the fire and attempt to answer the second question first…who is God? The dictionary defines God as "the creator and ruler of the universe; Supreme being"…pretty good definition, but should we elaborate? Yes, we should!

Again, these are Bob's thoughts on God and I am not trying to inflict my ideas and beliefs on you. I just want you to THINK! God is an all-knowing spirit, without shape, gender, race, or creed. Being God He (or She) existed in time and space for eons doing whatever Gods do, knowing everything and knowing everything that was happening and that which was going to happen. One day God became bored (yes I believe even God has bad days) and decided to create something that would challenge even His all-knowing powers and thereby inject a degree of uncertainty and excitement into His here-to-fore predictable existence. After just another day of creating The Earth and its birds, animals, and all the rest, He created his MASTERPIECE of NEVER ENDING UNCERTAINTY—-Man and then Woman. He then gave them free will to determine what they would do in their day-to-day lives. God has been sitting back and observing ever since that day relishing in the total never ending array of uncertain behaviors. For the most part, I am sure we disappoint God because, after all She is perfect in all things even in creating an imperfect species called humans and we (by design) are subject to our own free will and, therefore, that results in an infinite number and type of imperfections. What a wonderful, beautiful dichotomy…to be omnipotent and yet to create something that has the ability to cause you continual consternation and delight. But that, after all, was Her desire.

Now to further complicate things, we humans can't even decide on whether or not to put ketchup or mayonnaise on a hot dog. If that is true, and it is, how could we ever think that we could agree on anything, much less religion? Religion is a holy thing even if it is the atheistic religion. Even the atheists hold their beliefs sacrosanct and are willing to fight to the death with anyone who doesn't buy into their beliefs. My real problem with every atheist I have ever debated is that I get them so stirred up that they scream at me using the G__D____ epitaph. And they scream it louder and louder until I get their adrenaline around the boiling point. At that moment, I tell them the debate is over and start to leave, I then turn around looking at them with their smug faces (thinking that they have run me off) and I simply ask...Which God? Nothing more need be said.

That is enough of the atheists. We need to now shift our attention to one religion and that focus will, in all likelihood, cause a great deal of unrest in the readers of this book. That religion is the Muslim religion of Islam. Why am I focusing on this religion?—Because if we (religions other than Islam) do not immerse ourselves into learning all about this religion, our very existence is in jeopardy. Why do I make such an emphatic statement?—Because Islam is the religion of over forty percent of the world's population. But numbers alone do not cause a problem for the remainder of the world. The very real problem is the fact that Islam's bible, the Koran, is open to enormous variances of interpretation that have allowed radical elements within the Muslim communities to introduce sweeping, revolutionary, misleading interpretations of the Words of Muhammad. After all, everything I have read shows how very proud the Muslims are of the purity and the constancy of Muhammad's words from 500 a.d. to the current printings of the Koran. The problem with saying ANYTHING negative about Islam or the Koran or Muslims in general is that they all take their religion and religious beliefs much more seriously than do we of other religions. They are actually willing to sacrifice all (even if it means laying down their lives) and fight to the death in defense of their religion...and that "in defense of" can mean even a cartoon of Muhammad in a Danish newspaper. Now we Christians, on the other hand, don't take fun being poked at Jesus as anything but poor taste. Very few of us would perform suicide bombings for such an act...although it might show up on one of the late night TV shows as a comedy routine. Even when the MT's started their subtle attacks on our religious fabric by introducing the word "holiday" so we would not use the words "holy days" and the insidious "Xmas" (for convenience so as not to take up too much space in advertising) for "Christmas. HOW VERY THOUGHTFUL THESE MT BASTARDS ARE!!! Think!!! THINK!!! NOT WITH YOUR CHRISTIAN FORGIVING HEART BUT WITH YOUR BEAUTIFUL GOD GIVEN BRAIN!!! But I ask you, where are these progressive MT's with glorious rhetoric about (as per their point of view) necessary changes to anything Islam? Or are they so afraid that they might suffer the same fate as Salman Rushdie, the world famous author from England (born in India) who dared to write negative remarks about Islam. In answer to his writings, the orthodox Iranian leadership issued a "fatwa"against Rushdie on Valentines Day, 1989. Hardly a loving valentine...a fatwa is effectively a death sentence. If ANY MUSLIM kills Rushdie, (the killer) he is offered a large bounty on earth and a preferred place in the here after for himself and his family. To date, 18 years later, the fatwa has not been carried out...primarily because Mr. Rushdie is in hiding somewhere in England under the protection of the British government and police.

I am not saying to fear Muslims...I am saying we MUST gain a thorough understanding of all facets of the Muslim religion. It is not like being a Methodist where you go to church once a week, have bible study, sing a few songs, then forget the religion until the following Sunday. That to the vast majority of us is religion...a cursory attempt at religion that satisfies our need to say "I am a Christian, I go to church, so I will go to heaven." Sure some of us practice our religions with more energy and reverence, but we are absolute neophytes in our religious practice when compared to Muslims. To Muslims their religion is their lives...it is their alpha to omega...their very reason for being!

First of all, before I enter the world of Islam, I want to state that I AM NOT a scholar of this important religion. The opinions are my own, and, if I make mistakes or am in error, I will be pleased to retract any misinformation I state. If anyone has any problems, I will be pleased to sit down with that person, one-on-one in front of any audience as long as there is absolute decorum during the discussion. Also, if there are any questions in that forum that require a yes or no answer...that answer MUST BE A YES OR NO without further comment. If you do not agree, then do not presume to criticize my opinions. I likewise will operate under the same conditions.

The reason I am insisting on this type of format is...as I have inferred before...people have become expert in spinning answers, misdirecting meanings, avoiding true answers by interjecting other content, and various other actions. In other words, they use NLP and other techniques such as "talking points" to confuse and make everyone doubt that is really is is! They speak in convoluted rhymes, raising their voices to a deafening crescendo culminating in an ear-piercing diatribe of nonsensical faulty logic.

The major obstacle that anyone will have when trying to discuss or argue with any Muslim why he or she is not a Muslim, or does not believe in Islam, or just simply opts to take another religious road, is the fact that all Muslims believe that we are born as Muslims. This information sprang off the pages of Abdul A'la Mawdudi's book "Toward Understanding ISLAM" pages 4-10. When describing the aspects of man's life he states, "Like all other creatures man is born Muslim." I wasn't; how about you? The problem is that this is in their belief system. This is a MAJOR stumbling block for the hope of any compromise or understanding between Muslims and the rest of us.

Further in the Forward of this book, written in 1993 by Muhammad Fayyaz Khan, he writes, "For non-Muslims, the book holds a clear message, glad tidings, and a WARNING: study the fundamentals of Islam with an open mind, free of prejudice. But if, having understood its message you still reject it simply through stubborn prejudice, be prepared for tough accountability in the court of Allah and the Hereafter." Now remember, this is not like one of our preachers saying,

"You'll go to Hell if you do———." This is serious stuff to all Muslims and we need to understand the religious fervor that they place in their beliefs. Most writings are fear-based and carry dire consequences to all who do not believe and comply with completely. It is all-or-nothing! We, the infidels are the "nothing" because we have strayed from our Muslim beginnings and must suffer the consequences of our indiscretions. Their ALLAH is right and our GOD is wrong!

Later in the same book, pages 99 to 102, Mr. Khan has a section on "FAITH IN GOD'S PROPHETS" where he states that there have been 124,000 Prophets that have been sent to different people at different times. Further, he says that the Prophets mentioned in the Qur'an are required to be believed, but the remainder in India, China, Iran, Egypt, Africa, Europe, and other parts of the world aren't on the same level because they weren't mentioned in the Qur'an. PROBABLY, it would have been fairly difficult for these sub-Prophets to be mentioned in the Qur'an because most of them arrived many, many years after the Holy Qur'an was written which must have been around 600 AD because Muhammad was born on April 20, 571 AD.

While the Muslims pay lip service to the other Prophets and sub-Prophets, they denigrate and minimize the importance of all of the rest thereby exalting the ONLY TRUE PROPHET. Despite stating on page 100 that there is no difference between these prophets and Muhammad in the sense that all were sent by God as His Messengers and all were teaching the same straight path of "Islam." the author states that there are three differences between Muhammad and the other Prophets:

1. The other Prophets came to certain people for specific periods, while Muhammad was sent for the whole world, and all time to come.

2. The teaching of these Prophets have either completely disappeared from the world or whatever remains of them is not pure, and is found intermingled with many false and fictitious statements. Muhammad (peace be on him), therefore, is the only one of the whole line of Prophets who is a living personality and in whose footsteps it is possible to follow correctly and

confidently...(some of us who have been completely mislead by the teachings of that pretender Prophet Jesus Christ MIGHT DISAGREE VEHEMENTLY with Mr. Khan).

3. The guidance imparted through the earlier Prophets was not complete and did not cover all the necessary fields. Every prophet (notice how Mr. Khan suddenly lowers the case from Prophet) was followed by another who made alterations and additions in the teachings of his predecessors....At last, the most perfect system of guidance was given to mankind through Muhammad and all previous codes were automatically abrogated. All others were abandoned because it is both futile and foolish to follow an incomplete system while the complete one exists.

If all this self-serving, righteous extolling of the total perfection of the Prophet Muhammad to the total detriment of all the other "prophets" isn't disturbing to ANY honorable, God-fearing person, what am I missing? And how can anyone who says he or she is committed to the Creator, and professes complete submission and obedience to God, say that everyone whose beliefs aren't in tandem with his or hers is doomed to the fires of Hell?

We need to make one thing "perfectly clear," and that is Muhammadism is a misnomer for Islam and offends its very spirit since the Prophet Muhammad was a messenger of God and not a divine being worshipped by Muslims. So when we speak of the religion, we must use the proper word Islam. We outsiders are easily confused about Islam because we look at things (life, religion, politics, work, and even recreation) from an entirely different perspective than Muslims. To us, we segment all of our lives into various parts and each part is not interdependent upon another part. We separate Church from State; we go to church primarily on Sunday; we go to work and seldom think of our religion at work; and on and on. However, the followers of Islam carry their religion with them everywhere, and it is an essential part of every facet of their lives from birth to death and beyond.

In order to further understand our differences (and

I believe the only way to hopefully coexist is for us all to understand one another) is to go back to Mr. Mawdudi's book to page 44 and read the section III. THE PROPHETHOOD OF MUHAMMAD. In the beginning of this section, Mr. Mawdudi describes a situation that existed before the birth of Muhammad. "Great nations of the world were struggling hard to gain world supremacy, and in this long and ceaseless struggle, they exhausted all their resources and vitality. The Arabs were a fresh and virile people. So-called social progress had produced bad habits among the advanced nations, while among the Arabs no such social organization existed. They were, therefore, free from the inactivity, debasement and indulgences that luxury and sensual satiety lead to." He goes on to explain the noble qualities of the Arab people and the debasement of all other nations because of the evil influence of artificial social systems and civilizations. This reminds me of an old Mac Davis country and western song..."Oh Lord, it's hard to be humble when you're perfect in every way." Perfection is such a heavy burden!

Needless to say, if this is only a small portion of how the Muslims view the rest of us, no wonder we can't find any common ground for a symbiotic existence. Now remember that the Islamists take everything quite literally (especially when it suits their purpose) and they believe the Qur'an is perfect and has remained in its current form, without change, since the day it was written. It is the uncorrupted word of God! Also remember that Muhammad (to Muslims) is like a combination of Jesus Christ, Abraham Lincoln, and any other person you might like to add to this list. Mr. Mawdudi states that the whole world was in disarray...there was evil everywhere and people in their decadent behavior worshipped stones, idols, trees, stars, everything conceivable except God.

I guess Mr. Mawdudi forgot about what had occurred in Christianity in the 570 odd years before Muhammad was born. But OF COURSE SILLY ME Christians and Jews are not Islamists so we are ALL WRONG. How can any religion be so myopic in its views that its followers believe that all of God's People who are not of the Islamic faith are WRONG? Where is all the peace and brotherhood? Where is the understanding? I am still confused because I was not born, raised, schooled, and indoctrinated (at least 5 times a day) into such a rigid religion. But surely there MUST BE some common ground...we can at least agree to disagree can't we?

Before we delve more deeply into areas of Islam that are given to a wide range of interpretation, I want to go out on a fairly brittle limb and debunk one of the misconceptions that a large number of Muslims have about Muhammad. After he received the word of Allah and those words were written down by his scribes (he required scribes because he was illiterate) into what became The Qur'an, Muhammad decided to send messengers to various areas of the world to offer the word of Allah to the rest of the known world. One of those messengers went to Egypt (which was primarily Christian) to spread the word. The ruler of Egypt sent the messenger back to Muhammad with four presents, one of which was a female slave named Maria. Muhammad freed the slave girl, married her, and they gave birth to their only son named Abraham. By this action, Muhammad gave example to his followers that Islam would not accept slavery AND that it was permitted for Muslims to marry Christians. By the way, they had a fairly long life together...and all during their marriage Muhammad never insisted that Maria convert to Islam.

Now rather than continue into areas that I am, admittedly, not qualified to explore, I am going to finish up this analysis of Islam by focusing on the "j" word...yes, jihad. This word sends chills up the spine of those who are not Muslim, and I am sure sends mixed signals to a large number of Muslims. The reason for all this consternation on both sides of the Muslim versus everyone else is the very real fact that no one can say what this word means to every one and also what it means from time to time or situation to situation. An analogous word in my language would be battle. What does battle mean? Battle means a struggle; a fight; a striving; or an encounter. Are all these evil or bad? No, they are not. But if I have indoctrinated you from birth that a battle is a fight, a fight to the death against all enemies, and that fight is a noble and righteous endeavor and looked upon as holy by God and by doing battle your place in heaven will be insured...WHAT DO YOU THINK YOU WILL DO WHEN A RELIGIOUS LEADER CALLS ON YOU TO BATTLE? Yes, you will go into battle fearlessly and without even thinking because you have been totally programmed (BRAINWASHING is another word designed to describe this programming) to carry out this RELIGIOUS COMMANDMENT THAT SAYS THOU SHALT KILL!!! No matter what any one tries to say or argue that "jihad" is as a noble, peaceful striving/struggle for things such as education, work, popularity, health, status, and so on, DO NOT BELIEVE this attempt at misdirection. THINK! When was the very first time you encountered the word, jihad? Was it in a party situation or at a social function or even a religious event, and what was the year that you first were introduced to jihad? I'll bet my Cadillac (and I love my Cadillac...1997 El Dorado, candy apple red) that you first heard the word jihad some time slightly after September 11, 2001...right?

In the brochure JIHAD EXPLAINED, published by The Institute of Islamic Information and Education, P. O. Box 410129, Chicago, Illinois 60641-0129, I found both sides of the story. Initially the brochure focuses on the struggling and striving, but later the more currently meaningful explanations surface. I digress to the videos we have all seen about the "special schools" for Islamic children...where we see 2, 3 and 4year- olds being taught (brainwashed) relentlessly day after day to Praise Allah AND HATE all non believers ESPECIALLY THE JEWS AND AMERICANS! This is the END GAME for the extreme Islamics...The TOTAL ERADICATION OF ALL NON BELIEVERS!

Now, here come all the politically correct nitwits who think that what I have uncovered by reading Islamic books and brochures is utter nonsense. They are WRONG! They will say this is only indicative of a small fraction of the Islamic people. Well, bully for them, they are probably right, but I ask, "WHERE ARE ALL THE GOOD Muslims?" Is their inaction an indication of their true belief that the extremists are doing the good works of Allah or is their inaction a result of fear? We need to find out, but it is my personal belief that it is FEAR that precludes 98% of the world's Muslims from coming out against these diabolical maniacs. These guys would kill their own mothers or sisters and a few Imams if it suited their purpose. Along the way, they could also blow up a few mosques or maybe a couple of towers in lower Manhattan. THAT IS JIHAD! THINK!! Before it is too late—Stop turning the other cheek or you might not have any cheek (or maybe your whole body) left. THINK AND THEN THINK AGAIN AND AGAIN!!!

To totally put this one sided approach from the Muslims (yes even the moderate Muslims) in perspective, they expect and even demand equality when they enter our societies. They want all our laws to protect them (as they should IF they become citizens of America) and ensure their civil rights even to the point of wanting our system of laws to change to fit their beliefs (Sharia law). To heck with you Americans, we are here now and expect (yes demand) that YOU change to our better way! They want to foment divisiveness and unrest by having public meetings denigrating our country; they want to build their mosques in any area they wish; they want, they want, they want. Much of this is understandable in our democratic form of government. But if they want to change so much, why did they come here in the first place? They come to our country and want us to change to fit their previous way of life? WRONG!!! That just isn't the way it works, no matter how politically incorrect it might seem to them and the liberal advocates. If this continues, and the ACLU continues to back these demands to change our country and way of life to suit the Muslim life style, and they keep winning their suits, pretty soon it won't be the ACLU but the ICLU (Islamic Civil Liberties Union), and behind the liberal judge's bench, the sign will read IN ALLAH WE TRUST.

Now contrast this scenario with the converse. If we move to their country (for instance Saudi Arabia), even if we were allowed to become citizens, we would still not be allowed to participate in their legal system, we could not aspire to any level of authority in their government, we would not be allowed to build our own churches, we could not hold public rallies decrying our frustration with the government, and our women would have to dress according to Muslim etiquette. SOUNDS FAIRLY ONE SIDED doesn't it? It sounds that way because it is. But we sit back in our pious recliners, drinking our beers, watching the Super Bowl and eating burgers and chips, while the Muslims are busy little bees finding new and better ways to use our open, understanding, loving, and forgiving nature against us to achieve their END GAME. What is their END GAME??? Begin reading for yourself, and STOP LISTENING TO the alphabet 6 o'clock news liberals and reading the ultra liberal Old York Times. You might even finally ask your selves, where will my First Amendment rights and my freedom of speech rights be when Allah supplants God in America. THINK BEFORE YOU LOSE EVERYTHING, FOR God's sake THINK BEFORE IT IS TOO LATE!!!

The Muslims say that they are a loving, kind, benevolent, and forgiving people; HOWEVER, where are all these loving Muslims when there are horrific, inhumane events such as The World Trade Center Towers destruction carried out in the name of Islamic Jihad? The moderate Muslims say that only a small radical minority is to blame for these atrocities. If that is true, where are the priorities and voices and words of the vast majority condemning these Qur'an spinners? Yes, even Islam has its own Kennedy and Franken types. To all you moderate Muslims I say, you owe it to your dignity and pride and your God to take a stand against your evil brothers. Remember, their plan is when they finish with us...you will be next on their list of "disobedient folk." The Qur'an addresses those who claim to be believers: "O you who believe! Choose not your fathers nor your brethren for protectors if they love disbelief over belief; whoever of you who takes them for protectors, such are wrongdoers. Say: if your fathers, and your children, and your brethren, and your spouses, and your tribe, and the wealth you have acquired, and business for which you fear shrinkage, and houses you are pleased with are dearer to you than ALLAH and HIS MESSENGER and striving in His way: then wait till ALLAH brings HIS command to pass. ALLAH does not guide disobedient folk."

9:23, 24.

As further justification and rationalization for their evil acts, if you read the Qur'an with evil intent, (as written in <u>JIHAD EXPLAINED</u>, published by The Institute of Islamic Information and Education), the Qur'an permits fighting to defend the religion of Islam and the Muslims. This permission includes fighting in self-defense and for the protection of family and property. The early Muslims fought many battles against their enemies under the leadership of the Prophet Muhammad; the Muslims fought to defend their faith and community. The Qur'an adds: "Fight in the cause of ALLAH against those who fight against you, but do not transgress limits. Lo! ALLAH loves not aggressors....And fight them until persecution is no more, and religion is for ALLAH. But if they desist, then let there be no hostility except against transgressors." 2: 190-193.

Other areas of the Qur"an that illustrate the (if read with evil intentions) way many of the Imams and clerics choose to interpret Muhammad's words with a warlike aggressive bent are as follows: ALLAH orders the Muslims in the Qur'an: "If you fear treachery from any group, throw back (their treaty) to them, (so as to be) on equal terms. Lo! ALLAH loves not the treacherous." 8:58. Even the Prophet Muhammad undertook a number of armed campaigns to remove treacherous people from power and their lodgings. In His responsibility to protect His people and the religion He had established in Arabia, even He found it difficult to mobilize people to fight when they saw no invaders, but when He received intelligence reports about enemies gathering near His borders He carried out preemptive strikes, broke their power and dispersed them. ALLAH ordered Muslims in the Qur'an: "Fighting is prescribed upon you, and you dislike it. But it may happen that you dislike a thing which is good for you, and it may happen that you love a thing which is bad for you. And ALLAH knows and you know not." 2:216.

The brochure that I have quoted (<u>JIHAD EXPLAINED</u>), finishes up with a concluding thought: "Did Islam spread by force, swords, or guns? The unequivocal and emphatic answer is NO! The Qur'an declares: Let there be no compulsion (or coercion) in the religion (Islam). The right direction is distinctly clear from error. In conclusion, jihad in Islam is striving in the way of ALLAH by pen, tongue, hand, media and, if inevitable, with arms. However, jihad in Islam does not include striving for individual or national power, dominance, glory, wealth, prestige, or pride."

Now, to really nail this argument that Islam is a religion that has its roots in Silm and Salam which means peace for ALL GOD'S creations...A Muslim is supposed to live in peace and harmony with all God's creations. Islam protects all noble values and human rights; freedom, equality, justice, and the right to life, liberty and security of person are of prime concern in Islamic law: "Whosoever kills a human being for other than manslaughter or corruption in the earth, it shall be as if he had killed all mankind, and whosoever saves the life of one, it shall be as if he had saved the life of all mankind..." 5:32. This, to me, does not seem to be the outline for actions of some Muslims such as Ben Laden, al-Zawahiri, and some others, but to be ever more tolerant and understanding, I go back to one of the chief architects and leaders of contemporary Islamic resurgence, Mr. Abu A'la Mawdudi. This noted author and founder of Jamaat Islam suffered for years in a Pakistani prison, sentenced to death but that sentence was commuted to life imprisonment. He has authored more than one hundred works on Islam which have been translated into more than forty languages. You must admit, this man has impressive credentials.

In his own words, in his popular book TOWARDS UNDERSTANDING ISLAM, he states: "Islam" is an Arabic word meaning submission, surrender, and obedience. As a religion, Islam stands for complete submission and obedience to God. Since all created things obey the law of God, the entire universe, therefore, literally follows the system of Islam (FAIRLY SELF SERVING THESIS...don't you agree?). The sun, the moon, the earth, and all other heavenly bodies are thus "Muslim." So are the air, water, and soil, and all living things, the insects, birds and mammals of the animal world, the shrubs, trees, vegetables and fruits of the plant world. Everything in the universe is "Muslim."

Mr. Mawdudi continues on for another fifty pages explaining how Muhammad, after years of observing the corruption and decadence of the world around him, went into seclusion and fasted to purify his heart and soul even further. And Lo, when he awakened from his deep pondering, he saw how he might bring about the downfall of the corrupt and disorderly world and lay the foundations for a new and better one. Mr. Mawdudi incorporates all the teachings of Muhammad into the thesis that even though defense of Islam IS NOT a fundamental belief, its importance has been repeatedly emphasized in the Qur'an and Sunnah. He states, "It is essentially a test of our sincerity as believers in Islam. If we do not defend a friend of ours against plots or assaults from his enemies, nor care for his needs, we are indeed false pretenders of friendship;...Jihad is a part of this overall defense of Islam. Jihad means to struggle to the utmost of one's capacity. A man who exerts himself physically or mentally or spends his wealth in the cause of God is indeed engaged in jihad. But in the language of the Divine Law, this word is used specifically for the war that is waged solely in the name of God against those who perpetrate oppression as enemies of Islam. This supreme sacrifice is the responsibility of all Muslims. If, however, a section of the Muslims offer themselves for participating in JIHAD, the whole community is absolved of its responsibility. But if none comes forward, everyone is held guilty. This concession vanishes for the citizens of an Islamic State when it is attacked by a non-Muslim power. In this case, everybody must come forward for JIHAD. If the country attacked does not have enough strength to fight back, then it is the duty of the neighboring Muslim countries to offer help. If even they fail, then the Muslims of the whole world must fight the common enemy. In all these cases, JIHAD is as much a primary duty as are daily prayers or fasting. One who avoids it is a sinner. His every claim to being a Muslim is doubtful. He is plainly a hypocrite who fails in the test of sincerity and all his acts of worship are a sham, a worthless, hollow show of devotion.

The preceding paragraph should open your eyes if you are one of those Christians or other religious groups whose Pollyanna attitude is...this is a passing thing and it will go away, or these are just a misdirected minority of the Muslims, or "it's all good," or acunamatata. Guys, get a grip on reality!!!!! THINK!!!!!—BEFORE THERE IS A MOSQUE ON EVERY STREET CORNER AND YOUR WIFE IS WEARING A HAJIB OR A BURQA.

Again, these are my thoughts and if anyone wishes to discuss differences of opinion, I would be honored to be exposed to your constructive criticism...after all, as I have indicated earlier, I am not a scholar of any religion and have come to my conclusions independent of anyone's influence. I only used printed materials from reliable Islamic sources. Please show me where I am mistaken. I want to believe that a religion that has billions of followers and worshipers is a loving, caring, and forgiving religion...one in which 99.999% of its membership condemns the atrocities that Al Sadr and Hamas and Hezbollah have inflicted on totally innocent men, women, and children around the world in the name of Muslimic JIHAD. Do Not remain silent...speak up loudly and proudly. Be the Muslims Muhammad described that existed in Islam's GLORY DAYS (500AD through the 1100's).

PLEASE read your Qur'an. This great religious work tells you (all Muslims) to THINK for yourself and read into the words the spirit of The Creator. Words are only words and they can be misinterpreted by anyone, BUT the spirit of The Creator's words is eternally true.

Remember the old saying...LET NO GOOD DEED GO UNPUNISHED! I have several wonderful examples that should make you pause. You remember the tsunami in the Indian Ocean a few years ago? There was an enormous loss of life of the predominately Muslim population in the areas affected and billions of dollars of damage. Guess who was FIRST IN LINE TO OFFER, ARRANGE, AND DELIVER RELIEF

MEASURES???? Yes, it was the GREAT SATAN...the United States of America showing up with money, food, clothing, people, and materials necessary to help these unfortunates to begin their arduous recovery. Where was Iran, Syria, Palestine, and other Islamic countries? All they do is sit back and pay lip service to their fellow Muslims AND allow the infidels to draw down their wealth to (as they believe) weaken us even more. I ask you, where were the noble, honorable Iranians when hurricanes Rita and Karla devastated our country??? And when did Imam El Sadar say even one good thing about the US's humanitarian efforts or any other Muslim clerics throughout the Middle East or Indonesia or in Detroit? To the best of my investigation (which I have to admit is not world class), there were only four mentions of America's eleemosynary efforts and that was in obscure newspapers. What about Al Jazeera? They have learned from The Old York Times and the alphabet networks how to exploit and accentuate the negative and eliminate or diminimize the positive.

The Islamic religion teaches pride...pride in their religion, their families, their jobs, and pride in all their acts carried out in the name of ALLAH. That pride is a wonderful thing and should be commended. But I am confused. If these Islamic terrorists are carrying out their JIHAD in the name of ALLAH and they are proud of their efforts...WHY IN THE NAME OF ALLAH DO THEY ALWAYS COVER THEIR FACES? The terrorists sneak around capturing people, put the prisoners on camera making them decry their native countries and admitting their sins, then they cut their heads off. And all the while, they stand there with faces covered. This is the act of COWARDS, COWARDS who are afraid of being recognized. We would like to have them come on camera full faced so we can give them all the credit cowards and murderers are due. Shame on you...I do not believe your God would be very proud of you or your actions!

The MOST DISTURBING FACET OF OUR VIEW OF THE ISLAMIC RELIGION is the suicide bomber. Our religion glorifies life and if you live a loving, caring Christian life you will earn God's promise that you will ascend into heaven and your soul will exist forever in God's heavenly kingdom. If you take your own life, you have committed a sin that cannot be forgiven and one that will condemn your soul to an eternity in Hell. We are confused and don't have a reference point to be able to even remotely understand a religion that encourages its members to commit the ultimate sacrifice in the name of their God. How can this be love?

To finish up, I wanted to say a few things about another member of The Axis of Evil—North Korea. What about the human condition in North Korea? The general population lives in hovels and has a maximum of 2 cups of rice per day. The workers work joyously for the state, and the state provides.......... what? Not much! Only the elite have what we would consider a moderate lifestyle. The vast majority of the proud Korean people will NEVER own an automobile. All the country's moneys go to the pleasure of Kim Jong Il and his insane nuclear weapons projects...what about your people Kim? Or is this weirdo not so dumb and only playing us again to get more much needed food and fuel as blackmail payoff? Why do you spend millions on weapons and only thousands on food for your people...what a wonderful leader...by the way, who does your hair? So what happens when the Korean people are starving or need heating oil (where is Hugo?). The good old United States of America comes to the rescue again BUT GETS NO KUDOS...what's wrong with our public relations efforts? Remember, no one cares if they do not know! Fear not, the good old United Nations is always around to accept all the glory. Please don't forget the UN...the savior of the world or rather the savior of Kofi Annan, the bottomless pit of corruption and ineptitude. Enough of my waxing sarcastic, the people of North Korea receive the food and clothing but who knows if they really benefit from our benevolence? Do we receive any credit whatsoever? NO! We are still the Imperialistic Toothless Tiger to all those poor souls... and their hate continues, fed by Kim's propaganda factory. There is nothing wrong with taking credit for good deeds. The US needs to learn how to toot its own horn in a constructive manner; otherwise, no one will understand the caring, loving nature of the American People.

I want you all to know that when I say something derogatory about a country like Iran, Syria, and Korea, I am speaking about that country's leaders NOT the general population. It is my belief that the majority (the vast majority...maybe even 99%) of every country's citizens are just like you and me. All any of us want is to earn a good living for ourselves and our families, and we DON'T CARE one iota about all this B.S. perpetrated upon us by our leaders. Of course, we need leaders and governments BUT guys, get a life! PLEASE THINK!! PLEASE THINK ABOUT US!!!!

SPORTS AND AL'QUEDA

What, might you ask, do Sports and Al'Queda have in common or why are they even in the same chapter? I may be stretching things a little bit but bear with me and I'll try to put it all in perspective.

As I was reviewing all I could about the current world and its situations in preparation for writing this book (to my limited abilities), I had an inspiration. I was switching between Fox News and CNN watching O'Reilly, Hannity and Colmes, and Glenn Beck covering the world, as we know it, and various sports channels when I had a flash of creative brilliance. That flash gave me some insight as to similarities and differences between American Sports and Al'Queda. This is thinking "out of the box" but at least I am THINKING!

I started off sitting in my favorite overstuffed chair with a remote in one hand and a sandwich with chips and hot sauce and an ice cold Bud Light in the other hand (my other hand is fairly dexterous) watching the Super Bowl between The Colts and Da' Bears. The rain was pouring down and I just knew Da' Bears were going to kill The Colts in an open stadium on wet grass. As the game progressed, I began to doubt my prognostication as Payton began to impress his will (and talent) on the tiring Bears. All of a sudden the game was over and The Colts had won the Super Bowl and Payton was MVP. How glorious for The Colts and how disappointing for The Bears.

These teams, like the other 30 odd teams in the NFL, had pushed themselves to the maximum (I guess most of the other teams didn't push quite as hard) in order to achieve the FINAL VICTORY. Year after year, from the days these men were little boys with dreams of being the best in any sport, be it football, baseball, basketball, hockey, soccer, boxing, track and field, or anything else, they sacrificed mind and body and sometimes family, friends and even education to win that FINAL VICTORY. With the game over, I started to change channels to my favorite news channel when my revelation occurred.

At that exact moment it came clear to me the commonality between sports in America and Al'Queda. They BOTH want to achieve THE FINAL VICTORY at all costs. Both are dedicated to that goal. Each is willing to train ceaselessly to gain the physical and mental edge over the opponent (enemy) to prevail. The one major difference between the two organizations is... how does each organization define THE FINAL VICTORY?

A sports team is an assembly of individuals from different backgrounds and geographic environments. A head coach who is supported by assistant and specialty coaches leads the team. Every coach has his own area of expertise and together under the leadership of the head coach the team develops a strategy to defeat the specific opponent. While the coaches are developing the "game plan," the combatants are readying their bodies and minds in preparation for the mighty struggle. Finally, the big day comes and the two finalists line up mano a' mano in a mighty struggle that will leave one team defeated and one team experiencing THE FINAL VICTORY. That is the end game for American sports, BUT that is not exactly the mindset for Al Queda and the other terrorist groups throughout the world.

The Terrorist Brotherhoods (TB's) are basically the same as the sports teams with a few subtle differences. Actually, there are more than a few differences and they are NOT SUBTLE!

When I talk about TB's you must understand that terrorism is not relegated to one single group of idiots such as Al Queda. There is a lot of lunatic fringe groups located throughout the world, and yes, "dear hearts," some possibly in your own town or even in your neighborhood. They are not exactly linked at the hip but one thing is for sure...their goal is the complete eradication (yes, the blotting out; the extirpation; THE TOTAL EXTERMINATION OF EVERYONE WHO

DOES NOT BELIEVE EXACTLY AS THEY DO). This even holds true for any Muslim who does not fall into line! These groups had their start centuries ago, but the real impetus for the worldwide ferment of organized terrorism began in Iran with the ascension to power of the Iatola Komani in the mid-1970's. Under his fanatical leadership, the extremely radical element of militant Sunni Islamist organizations had their genesis supported by a religious zealot with lots of oil money to spend. The beautiful part of their worldwide plan "to eliminate foreign influence in all Muslim countries, eradication of those deemed to be infidels, elimination of Israel, and the creation of a new Islamic caliphate" was that they had all the time in the world to sow their seeds of social upheaval. No one, not even Interpol, MI-5, or the CIA, actually knew these organizations existed. True, they heard rumors, but no credence was given to these rag tag groups that were going to "take over the world...at least not until the late 1980's when more serious and reliable intelligence began to surface. Most of this intelligence focused on Afghanistan, Pakistan, Iran, Indonesia, Palestine, and The Sudan. Still, this was "stuff on the radar," so rather than taking this potential threat seriously and implementing some preventative medicine (i.e. eradication), the various intelligence services just sat back and observed and made some notes. This was a new type of threat (nothing serious like an entire country attacking), so these agencies did very little because they had no reference with which to compare. This lack of due diligence showed up as a glaring miscalculation when embassies, ships, hotels, towers, trains, and busses began to "blow up." What a beautiful game plan developed by head coaches Osama bin Laden and Ayman al-Zawahiri!...Lull your opponent to sleep, then throw the long ball and catch them off guard (with their pants down) and deal a lethal blow.

Now, let's get back to the major differences in this analogy. The sports enthusiasts begin at a young age, work hard at the local field or court, learn the rudiments of the game, get physically and mentally ready, wear easily identifiable uniforms that proudly display their team, play ever more serious games and at the end of each game the opponents congratulate each other for a game well played.

The TB's also start at a young age—a very young age. Even though neither bin Laden nor al-Zawahiri's backgrounds held scholarly qualifications for issuing Islamic edicts (fatwas), they took it upon themselves to issue their fatwa in 1996 which amounted to a "public declaration of war" against the United States and all who sided with the US. As part of this fatwa, children as young as three years of age were placed in a rapidly expanding network of radicalized Islamic schools called "madrassas" where the indoctrination (brainwashing) began. Please note...these are NOT SCHOOLS like my elementary school—Austin Elementary...these are the embryonic puppy mills for the TB's brave new world. These innocent children (they are no longer innocent after even a few days of intense indoctrination) are not taught the 3 R's. Rather, they are taught that everyone is their enemy or potential enemy, so the best thing is to trust no one except those in your class and your teachers. Do not trust even your own parents! DOES THIS REMIND YOU OF SOMETHING THAT HAPPENED IN THE 1930's and 1940's? THINK!!!!!REMEMBER!!!!! THEN THINK AGAIN!!!!!!!!!

The daily curriculum includes endless prayer sessions while kneeling and playing with their worry beads; periods of free speech where they are free to say anything they want...as long as it is restricted to Kill all American devils, Kill all Jews, Destroy all Infidels and ALLAH IS THE ONE AND ONLY GOD AND DEATH TO ALL WHO DO NOT BELIEVE. Other little tidbits surround the central theme that to die in the "defense" of Allah is a noble endeavor even if it means suicide. My question is a very simple one and one no one has asked before...if it is so glorious to die for Allah, and the people who die for Allah and their families receive eternal benefits in heaven alongside Allah, why don't bin Laden, al-Zawahiri and the other honorable leaders take a page from their own book and go and BLOW THEMSELVES UP? Or maybe these guys don't like virgins. Am I right Osama? Crawl out of your cave and tell all your followers who keep covering their faces when they behead someone or blow up innocent people (infidels as well as fellow Muslims) that Now is the time for Osama and "the boys" to take the final step...DO IT, BUT DO IT NOW...or are you just full of cowardly rhetoric? LEAD FROM THE FRONT O NOBLE ONE! Don't THINK; Just DO IT!

Now that the future players have finished high school and have graduated Magna Cum Blow Me Up, they are ready to go forth and destroy. They come from very diverse backgrounds and easily return to their native countries and blend in forming mole cells. These cells remain dormant for years. I do not mean inactive but they are not overt in their actions. The cell members get jobs, marry, have children, attend mosques, and never do anything that remotely resembles anything illegal or controversial. They ooze into their neighborhhods, and quietly have secretive meetings and conversations to stay razor sharp for the inevitable call to action. When the call comes, they are ready to spring into action and carry out the game plans that have been so laboriously designed to do the most damage and kill the maximum infidels possible. This is their Super Bowl and this is THE FINAL VICTORY that they have been working toward. BUT too bad, the one thing these godless devils (yes they claim to love Allah, BUT they love nothing and their Allah lives in a cave in the Tora Bora Mountains of Afghanistan/Pakistan) forgot was the indomitable spirit of the American people. Poor accommodations for a god, but he deserves the very best.

America's poorest school district and America's least successful sports franchises have a set of noble goals and God willing, one day their honest efforts will bear fruit and they will tread on the field or court to compete for a district or world championship. Conversely, the TB's one day, allah bin Laden willing, will crawl out of their cells with their faces characteristically covered because they are ashamed of themselves, stand up on their two cloven hoofs, and skulk out to kill or maim innocent men, women or children because they can't do anything constructive just like the Muslims of the Dark Ages of Islam in the 1000's-1200's A.D could do nothing.

I say Muslims of the world UNITE against these cowardly maniacs and renounce them and their malignant ideology that is a blasphemy to your religion and to ALLAH. They are the INFIDELS!

SEX

This subject stirs more emotion than anything else in the human world. Why? After all, it is the God given method of procreation of the species, isn't it? It is really that simple and this could be the shortest chapter in any book ever written, EXCEPT for the fact that the human animal has morphed this beautifully loving and caring essential function into many forms from an exciting interaction between partners to a disgusting, degrading activity that would make the Marques d' Sad repel with revulsion.

It is my firm belief that the main reason sex is easily perverted is the fact that parents don't take the time to sit down with their children to have a one-on-one private discussion about a normal bodily function. The mothers and fathers just sit back and hope their children learn "the right way or in the converse…if they learn the wrong way, hopefully nothing too bad will happen." WHAT'S WRONG WITH YOU MOTHERS AND FATHERS??? Are you just stupid or do you just not care? I have been blessed with only one child, but you can be sure that from the time she was eight years old, we had progressively more and more detailed discussions about her sexuality. There was NEVER any discussion about THE BIRDS AND BEES! How very dumb and stupid do you think your children are? The real question is…how dumb and stupid are you? Actually, I don't believe you parents (not All, but a Large number) are stupid, but I do believe you are lazy and put your children's healthy life and safety far behind your own precious feelings. Too bad your parents didn't provide you with sex education, but for God's sake, now is the time to break this cycle of ignorance. If you do this for your children, you will drive the pimps and whoremongers out of business and you will shut off the supply of innocent, vulnerable children from the predatory maggots of our society (i.e. Pedophiles). If there were one group that I could eliminate from the face of the earth, it would be pedophiles.

I won't even write their descriptive word again because it revolts me to even think that people of this ilk are allowed to even breathe the same air, drink the same water, see the same stars, or play in the same parks with the rest of us. You may think what I am about to say is inhumane, but again, these are my thoughts. I believe anyone who is convicted of these acts should suffer immediate (not endless years of incarceration) execution. And if you think that is "cruel and unusual punishment," YOU ARE RIGHT! The only problem I have with this punishment is that there is not enough pain and it is over too soon. If you bleeding heart, stupid, unfeeling liberal idiots wish to debate this subject...I say ANY TIME ANY WHERE if we are in the public eye so you can exhibit your understanding and love of our most precious possession—our children. If you can't see your way to killing these worthless scum, I have an alternative. We will give them an alternative to the death penalty...one year... yes one year in stocks. They can opt to eliminate execution by allowing themselves to be locked in stocks in a public square 18 hours per day for one year. The people of that community would be allowed, without fear of reprisal or legal action, to humiliate them in any manner that fits the crime.

NEWS FLASH, NEWS FLASH...today (February 23, 2007) the ex President of the ACLU...Yes I said the ex President of the ACLU has been arrested in his home by ICE (an international watchdog whose charter is to identify child abusers and pedophiles in every country of the world and bring them to justice). He is accused of possessing extremely offensive videos of young girls (under 12 years of age) restrained and being raped. GOOD WORK ICE!!!!! I was right earlier when I nick named the ACLU the American Criminal Liberties Union. You guys should be commended for your thorough background checks on employees, especially for your top dog. Maybe, just maybe, you guys have a new "innocent" potential client and you can set a new precedent for the rights of sex deviates. If you do, it is my hope you and yours become involved with these perverts because "if you sleep with dogs, you get fleas." THINK!

The reason I feel so strongly about this subject is the fact that once a person's innocence has been violated, that person's life, hopes, and dreams are over. And all who come in contact with that person are also adversely affected...and so on, and so on, and so on until the end of time. I can hear the outcry now from the liberal lunatic fringe...these people can be rehabilitated and made useful members of society. If you truly believe this tripe, I will change my stance and agree with you wholeheartedly IF after these maggots have been treated and cured (by your own criteria)...they come to live the rest of their lives in YOUR HOUSE! This sounds fair to me...if you talk the talk, you must also walk the walk. DEAL OR NO DEAL? Thought not you loud mouthed, squeaky speaking, liberal ignoramus.

The ability of the human animal to find ways to take a person into even deeper levels of decadence is only matched by the human nature to take everything down to its lowest base nature. Why is this? There are endless books and thoughts and studies that have been undertaken by thousands of knowledgeable scholars trying to describe or explain this anomaly and they have all come up with answers. The numbers of answers almost outnumber the grains of sand in an hourglass, BUT the real reason is THE MONEY and/or POWER.

We think that we are the superior animals on The Earth, BUT even the lowest of the low animals (even those who cannot reason) innately understand The Circle of Life. Luckily, the species that was created in God's image also has the ability to create ugliness where there is beauty, pain where there is happiness, and moral decay where there is purity...sure am glad we were made in God's image, if not, we could be in BIG TROUBLE! I am going to address just a few areas that I THINK need to be exposed to the light of reason: rape, prostitution, and pedophilia.

Rape (of a male or female) is an act of rage or hate or power. No matter what the excuse (there is NO reason for rape), the act is not only illegal but it is abhorrent to all INCLUDING the rapist. The person attacked is forever changed...he or she is damaged, the rape has violated the psyche, therefore the violator should either be put to death or, if you are one of those who do not believe in the death penalty, placed in stocks in the public square for one month. During that month, the citizens of the community will be allowed, without penalty) to impose any and all types of punishment on the rapist. If, after release, that individual rapes again, he or she will be executed after trial and conviction.

Prostitution is a money and/or power situation. The prostitute ends up in this situation for a multiplicity of excuses (I truly believe there is no reason to become a prostitute). Some people say that prostitution is a necessary evil, but by saying this they admit it is an evil, but they continue and say it serves a social need and should be made legal (more left wing liberal thinking about making everything legal, therefore there is no crime). Some idiots even say that this is a victimless crime—-WRONG! I watched a TV documentary the other day about prostitution (legalized) in Nevada. The reporter was interviewing the owner (pimp) and his stable of "working girls." All the girls had been in his employ for over five years and proudly stated that they enjoyed their work and one offered that she was a millionaire. Now realize, at no time were the girls with the reporter without the owner present...wonder why?

This owner further stated that all his girls are clean and are checked by a physician monthly...too bad, some STD's don't show up for months or even years with ordinary lab tests. He then stated that he was the wave of the future and that legalized prostitution for the entire U. S. was coming soon. Victimless crime??? All I know is that I have seen many resumes and not one of them had as occupation...PROSTITUTE...this despite their proclaiming that theirs is the world's oldest profession.

What can anyone say about pedophilia without wanting to run a stake through the heart of ANYONE who would harm an innocent child? If you feel otherwise, or if you try to rationalize any of these acts, or if you feel that there is any justification whatsoever in such an act, I encourage you to either commit suicide right now (yes, even before you finish reading my wonderful book...too bad I didn't include a suicide kit with the book—my error) or come to my home, and stay in stocks, that I will personally design and fit to your body size—no extra charge, for one month. During that month I will be the perfect host and cater to your every need.

Pedophilia is a crime in all (I believe) states, but the punishments rarely fit the crime. I guess about now the liberal masses are crying out, "there has to be some extenuating circumstances that caused this poor man to break the law, but even if there are no excuses, we should decriminalize this act to protect his CIVIL RIGHTS." Sorry guys, poor potty training or an unloving mother or being humiliated at school, and other humiliations are not a reason or defense. Also, I don't give a damn about his civil rights—he gave up his civil rights when he destroyed that child's innocence. Refer back four paragraphs to my thought on stocks and you will see my preferred method of dealing with convicted pedophiles. If any of you actually believe (not just being "politically correct") that there should be ANY understanding or forgiveness for this despicable act, I encourage you spread you body with honey and walk buck-naked into a huge fire ant colony and sit down for a day. You would be getting off easy as compared to the irreparable harm you have done to this child, his/her family and friends, his/her future children and their children's children. Once convicted, these maggots of society should be put to death, no excuses, and, if any judge allows these pariahs back on the streets before their entire sentence (albeit too little), the judge should be removed from the bench without recourse.

Don't get me wrong; I enjoy sex as much as anyone, but all things in moderation and at the right time with the appropriate person. A healthy sex life is normal and healthy for us humans. Where we go wrong is when we stray from (what I call, for the want of another term) the norm. Now hold on; I realize everyone's norm is different, BUT we can all (or most of us) agree that rape and pedophilia is not acceptable but can be described as abnormal and criminal. As long as the laws say something is acceptable to the nation, I will go along with that situation. Of course, if I feel differently, I have the right to act on behalf of my rights and feelings and, again, the nation will decide. Thank God we live in a country that allows anyone, no matter how deviant or outlandish the idea, to express his or her feelings and even put his or her ideas in front of the electorate (if you have enough deviants like yourself to get your proposition on a ballot). But do not give up hope; there is a glimmer of hope for all of you who are on the lunatic fringe...you have the Libertarians and the left wing liberal ST's who are trying to MAKE EVERYTHING LEGAL. Just think, if they have their way, you might have Charles Manson as your neighbor...FUN, FUN, and FUN! Helter-skelter every day!!!!!

I could go on and on with this subject, but why? This subject is far too personal for me, a white, divorced sixty-four-year old male to attempt or assume to tell you how to conduct your private lives. I could, but why try...you are going to do exactly what your conscience will allow you to. But remember, if you are heading toward experimenting with deviant sex, you can't just jump from normalcy to Bundy type exploits. You must, just like beginning a life of drug addiction, start with something light and without addictive qualities (YEAH RIGHT) like marijuana and slowly graduate to the really good stuff like black tar heroin or crack cocaine or ice. You parents need to take the bull by the horns and do what my parents did for us kids at a very young age (9 or 10) I believe.

I know for a fact that my parents had a very hard time dealing with the subject of sex. They fumbled around and finally got to the point with my older brother, then me and finally, the most difficult of all, my sister. But to their credit, they did it in a realistic manner (no birds and bees) and in a family situation. My brother and I thought it quite comical to see our parents telling us what we had already heard of from the "experts" at school, BUT when we were finishing my father said one thing that I have always carried with me and handed down to my daughter...ALWAYS REMEMBER THAT SEX IS

NOT A PLAYTHING, IT IS A BEAUTIFUL PART OF LIFE BESTOWED UPON US BY GOD. He also reminded us boys that a woman should always be respected and, if we respected her, respect would be returned. That was my first introduction to the theory of reciprocity. What a powerful tool...if you do something personal, significant, and unexpected for someone else, that person is obligated to do the same (or similar) for you. Try it sometime; you will be pleasantly surprised and astounded at the resulting response! THINK!!!

ILLEGAL DRUGS

Do not be fooled. It is not only the illegal drugs that can ruin your life. Prescription drugs can and usually are as addictive as their homegrown or bathtub cousins. The major difference is that prescription drugs have at least been laboratory tested for effects and side effects. But fear not, if you do not follow the label instructions, you will become addicted, become severely ill, or die.

Drugs are a subject that happens to be on the top of my mind. Drug traffickers are one of the lowest forms of the human animal. Think about it, they exist for only one reason... that being to get another human to try a drug for the first time. Once they have succeeded in step one, all the other steps are easy...another, then another until that precious, innocent trusting human is now hooked and for all intents and purposes his or her "normal" life is over. Please understand, when people decide to take that first hit, snort, injection, or pill, they have FORFIETED THEIR DIGNITY!

The rest of their life now has but one purpose—-to get high again and again. And when that high is not enough, there are even more drug sellers who will gladly introduce them to another, even more powerfully addictive substance. This spiral activity goes on in ever lower diminishing concentric circles until there is nowhere else to go. At that point, the only inevitable end is death. And this slide down the slippery slope of life has been greased by that first experimentation of a drug as seemingly innocent as marijuana or Xanax. Beware of those "innocent" drugs...they have very deadly friends at the end of the ride. THINK, FOR GOD"S SAKE THINK!! You are a beautiful person, with a long, productive life ahead of you. Sure, there are bad times ahead, maybe even bad times now, but that is what life is about. Your greatest attribute is your God given spirit. If you let it, that spirit will allow you to overcome all obstacles. Do not give up on life and DO NOT GIVE UP ON YOURSELF...you are too important for us to lose. THINK!

The drug dealers sit and wait as their current drug addicts go out and recruit new victims. The traffickers are smart...they first get the beautiful people hooked by preying on their insecurity and telling them these drugs will make them even more popular. Once they have these elite types hooked, they have a popularity driven sales force. To further show their brilliance, they realize no one wants to say I am hooked on dope, or I can't get through a couple of hours without a fix, or I inject a needle four times a day...THAT WOULD NOT BE ALLURING OR COOL. So these sewer scum come up with hip, descriptive words that take the potential (and current) victims' minds off the awful degrading nature of this social disease. Some of these hip terms are: shoot up, take it to the limit, blow your mind, Mary Jane, crystal, ice, and more. But no matter what the hip version is... the very real fact is that the product being sold is DOPE and the ones taking these substances are DRUG ADDICTS. Did you see the movie TRAFFIC starring Michael Douglas? If you have not seen this graphic movie, I suggest you put my book down right now and view this movie with your entire family... don't leave out the kids even if they are only eight or nine years old. After all, you will be right there with them to explain the rough parts.

Now that you are back, your are now more in tune with what I am attempting to get over to you...We are in a lot of trouble because we have too long allowed others their say about this topic: the liberal media types and entertainment types and fashion types from Janis Joplin to John Belushi; from TV network executives to Howard Stern; from Johnny Carson to David Letterman to Jay Leno making light of drugs in order to make an audience laugh—-shame on all of you! You people are or were media and entertainment icons...YOU HAVE

A RESPONSIBILITY TO THE AMERICAN PEOPLE, ESPECIALLY THE CHILDREN TO PLACE DRUGS WHERE THEY BELONG—-IN THE CATEGORY OF POISON!

Am I overreacting? No. Am I too conservative and protective of our children? No. Am I invading people's right to privacy? No. Am I attempting to somehow or another truncate "free speech"? No. Am I just a silly old sixty-four-year old man who isn't with it? Well maybe, BUT at least I care—which is more than I can say about a large number of parents over the last fifty years. THINK!!!!

Ask yourself, why?..................WHY WHAT? Why, if drugs are such a huge social problem, doesn't someone or some country or United Nations (NOT) take the initiative in the eradication of these insidious chemicals? I would venture a guess that if we focused on eliminating heroine, cocaine, and methamphetamines, and we were successful, we would see the following happen in the majority of the nations of the world... at least a 90% reduction in murders, rapes, robberies, car-jackings, assaults, and prostitution. Now ask yourself again why are the leaders of so many of the world's countries not attacking this problem with all the resources at their command? If my estimation was only one-half correct, the reduction in the cost of drug related arrests and prosecution and incarceration would be in the billions of dollars...isn't that enough incentive? Or... or...or...is it more profitable to those in high places to allow this social calamity to continue? THINK, THINK, THINK!!!

Am I inferring that corruption exists at high levels in major countries and even (GOD FORBID) in the United Nations? Of course, I'm not inferring anything of the sort...I am stating with every word in my mind that MONEY CORRUPTS and MONEY CREATES POWER and ABSOLUTE POWER CORRUPTS ABSOLUTELY!!! Yes there is corruption. Are you willing to take the low road and allow this malignancy to continue? Or do you have the integrity to do your best to turn this Soulless Train around?

If, as I have described, these substances are so bad and evil, why don't we just take the high road and eliminate them from the face of the earth? There are many reasons that drugs will always be a part of our lives, but for every good reason, there is a converse argument stating the horrendous effects on us. I will enumerate several reasons not to eradicate drugs and then I will follow up with a much longer list of reasons to eliminate the majority of them.

Almost from the beginning of man's memory, he has been searching for The Silver Bullet, The Philosopher's Stone, The Fountain of Youth, or some other magical way of eliminating the many real or imagined ills of man. Man (woman) also has other reasons to include drugs into his/her medicine chest of hope. Remember, if you are as old as I, the verse of The Rolling Stones hit—-"Mother's Little Helper"—-that states when things are hard she "goes running for the shelter of her mother's little helper; it helps her on her way, through each trying day." Now, this song came out in the mid 1960's when I was in my early 20's. It was a time for love and peace and drugs...in fact, one popular saying was "live fast, love hard and die young." Looking back now, it is evident that the majority of us were pretty much like today's youth, but there was, as today and I guess tomorrows also, an element in every era, a much smaller group that will experiment with anything We, the majority, went along for the ride, but never jumped on the drug train. The excitement of that era included concerts, riotous parties, love ins—all that included drugs...drugs that were intended to reduce our inhibitions and/or expand our senses so we could see the beauty of life, increase the fun of the sexual experience, drop out or even see God. Believe it or not, in the 1960's there was a song by a singer named Donovan that was titled Mellow Yellow. That song encouraged the use of banana peel as a drug either to be smoked or injected to achieve a high. HOW ABSOLUTELY STUPID CAN WE BE?

How very bad can someone's life be for them to seek escape by either stimulants or depressants?

My parents hate me;
My parents ignore me;
My parents try to control me;
My parents don't show me enough love;
My parents give me no respect;
My parents won't buy me a cell phone;
My parents won't buy me an Ipod;
My parents won't let me have my own computer;
My parents make me do chores;
My parents don't understand me;
I have too much homework;
No one likes me at school;
They give me energy;
They make me feel sexy;
They reduce my stress;
They make me forget about "the bomb."

There are probably fourteen thousand more very good reasons for drug use but I say cop out! These are not reasons... they are excuses! YOU are the answer to the drug problem. Yes, YOU, not the politicians with their hands out, not even the corrupt elite who think of nothing more than how they can make even more money at the expense of the pain and misery of the masses. No, I am not against all politicians or people who become wealthy from hard work or other noble means. I just believe that making money off the ignorance or misery of others less fortunate is wrong and there is no way anyone can try to rationalize this narcissistic greed.

Please don't delay one minute. Call a family meeting right now (lay the book down, what you are about to do is far more important than reading this book) and ask everyone for opinions on this subject. By asking, you might just be very surprised that your children have more answers than questions and even more questions than you. And they may have an even broader perspective on drugs than you can imagine. The main thing is that you have all taken the first step in not only a better life for you and your family but for your community, state, country and world. You can do it! Take the first step. THINK! YOU CAN AND WILL MAKE A DIFFERENCE! THINK!!!!!

If you cut off the demand, which I believe we will do when we take the proactive approach I have described, i.e., tighter nuclear families, more love, more touching, more understanding and more parental intervention, and more religious training for the whole family TOGETHER, you will impact what economists say is upstream management. In other words, the whole drug culture is nothing more and nothing less than SUPPLY AND DEMAND ECONOMICS. We all learned this in Economics 101, but I venture to say, the drug warlords learned it a little bit better than 98% of all Americans. For sure they have a good business plan and they have been implementing the plan and refining it for decades.

First, you find a poor country that has favorable soil and weather patterns, a corruptible political climate, and a work force that is barely making ends meet by growing normal agricultural crops. Next, you mingle, fit in, and show everyone how they can make more with less effort. Then you plant the seeds or vines and let nature take its course. While the crops are growing, you send a few emissaries to create the initial demand. That is the easiest part because there are always a few people who do not have or ever have had any real love and understanding and who have little or no religious anchors. These are the nucleus around which you build your drug empire because without demand the entire business plan fails. You can grow and process the world's most potent marijuana or the purest cocaine or concoct the most addictive methamphetamine possible, BUT without "recreational users"—- YEAH RIGHT...I AM NOT HOOKED, I JUST WANT TO GET HIGH OR TAKE THE EDGE OFF, OR IT MAKES ME FEEL SO SEXY AND POWERFUL, you go nowhere. You are right; you are not hooked...you are landed. And just like what happened to the salmon (when my daughter and I were lucky enough to go to Tikchik Narrows Lodge in Alaska)...we caught them, pulled them into the boat, then we hit them on the head with a club. The only difference between the salmon and the "not hooked addicts" is that the poor salmon are dispatched quickly out of their misery while the addicts linger for years and years denying reality until they reach their inevitable reward.

The "non-addicts" lie, steal, sell themselves for sex, and will even kill their own family members if that is what it takes to get that next high...which becomes ever increasingly harder to achieve. What to do when one line, one tok, or one needle isn't sufficient to get to that euphoric FIRST HIGH? The LOGICAL ANSWER (and you must understand these people are thinking logically...after all that's the reason they first started using drugs isn't it?) is to take a larger dose. If that does not work, and it won't for long, move up to an even more potent drug. When that fails to get that more and more elusive high, they can become chemists and mix the drugs...YEAH THAT'S THE ANSWER...why didn't I think of that before? Want to guess what the next step will be...? You are right; the next step will be into a coffin! But they are seeking a closer consciousness with spirituality, aren't they? Maybe that was the Pollyanna story they told themselves that first fateful day when they lost their dignity and their very soul. Sounds horrible, doesn't it? But fear not, the liberals will say all you have to do is send them to rehab and then EVERYTHING WILL BE OK...what? THINK!! Rehab IS NOT AN ANSWER; it is a band aide on a desecrated, wounded wretch who once was a dignified, self-respecting human being.

The actual cure rate (totally cured for more than five years) is less than 25%. This, my friends, is a lower success percentage than for people trying to kick Starbuck's, and much lower than those diagnosed with leukemia, liver cancer, prostate cancer, colon cancer, and many other diseases. Yeah, rehab is the answer to all ills: politicians who are pedophiles or accused of drunken driving; movie stars who stagger everywhere showing their private parts then show up after rehab totally shaven with tattoos, singers falling off the stage and forgetting their lines; and believe it or not the seemingly endless numbers of "men of god" energy reverends who feed off people's need to be told everything will be ok, ok if...if...if. One of those ifs is

IF you give enough when that collection/tithing plate comes around. MONEY can buy you happiness in the sanctuary of these DOCTOR FEEL GOOD GOSPEL SPOUTERS...ask them, they will tell you whatever your little empty heart wants to hear. Our newest fallen reverend in Denver is going through two or three separate rehabs for multiple transgressions. But I am confident that once he is HEALED, he will be back in some pulpit somewhere, telling everyone about how the DEVIL tempted him and he was weak and fell from grace. Skeptical me (I do honestly hope they are all cured) , but I would be willing to bet the farm that we will hear from them again as they once more are entering yet another rehab. I THINK WE SHOULD BUY STOCK IN REHAB.com;...it looks like a growth industry and a real money maker. THINK!!!

ILLEGAL IMMIGRATION

There is NOTHING wrong with immigration. Throughout time, people, who were not happy (for any number of reasons) living in their native country, packed up whatever worldly possessions they could carry and set off in search of a better life in a foreign land. To my way of thinking, these people were (are) very brave and adventurous and possibly fool hearty because (tragically) many of these travelers die in the attempt and a large number of these deaths are murders. Yes, their guides known as "coyotes" take their money then kill them during the trip. But to these people, the risk is worth taking when compared to their current situation.

One of the good things about America (there are many) is the fact that America is the land of the free and home of the brave and that self same freedom draws people from every nationality in order that they can have a fresh start...NEW BEGINNINGS. And the dream of new beginnings and a higher degree of freedom to achieve these dreams is the stuff that movies are made from.

We hear every day (you can not miss all the negative media because the media feeds off negative feelings and emotions) that the United States is racist, takes advantage of minorities and the poor, has a system that only benefits the elite—the wealthy, is fat and lazy...a toothless tiger, and is on its last waning years as a world super power much like Rome was before its demise. The press, TV, and radio hourly present the dooms day scenarios of "the end is near," BUT here they (immigrants from all over the world) come by the thousands every year. The last several years has produced a bumper crop from the immigrant tree with millions, like Neil Diamond so beautifully sang, "Coming to America." THINK!!! If this country has citizens from EVERY COUNTRY and only reports actual Native Americans numbering less than 2% of the total population, why do they keep coming? Because, my friend, we are the one single hope of the world. Sure we have problems but who doesn't and in spades! And problems and adversity is the challenge and fuel for our growth and success. Bring on the problems...we will solve them...as long as we pull together. So, all you liberals who only can find fault with The Mona Lisa, a Stradivarius cello, or The Statue of Liberty, GET ON BOARD OR GET OFF...there are plenty of immigrants anxious to take your place and make America an even better place. These people from down trodden existences are full of the energy and hope our ancestors brought with them. So I think it would be an excellent trade of one lone, hard working Mexican or Asian, or African for George Soros and all his billions, Alec Baldwin, Barbara Striesand, Ted Kennedy, and all those who have become fat and lazy and so full of free time that they have forgotten their own heritage and who (or what) they owe their success to! THEY OWE EVERYTHING TO AMERICA! If any one of you I've mentioned would like to debate this statement, I will make myself available...you pick the time and place and I'll be there. Ted, how successful do you think you would have been if you had been born in The Sudan? Now answer carefully and honestly before you take your next drink and begin huffing and puffing because people are beginning to think that trading Ted for Manuel is a good thing and better for America. THINK!!!!

We Americans are so very blessed that we were born here, so we easily become jaded and think what we have is normal, but it isn't. If you need a wakeup call, take a trip outside our borders not just to a third world country but a trip to France or Germany or Sweden or China and, when you return, you will thank the Lord you are an American. You will now understand why these "huddled masses" are yearning to breathe free.

We should not forget that for certain over 95% of current citizens of America come from immigrant stock...be it from

England, Ireland, Scotland, all the European and Scandinavian countries, Russia, the Baltic states, the middle eastern countries, the entire Orient, all of the African continent, Australia, Central and South America. If I have left any country out, it is not intentional. Enough said, the vast majority of the countries of the world have made significant contributions to America's citizenry capital and America is better for their presence.

Back in the "good old days," the numbers of these adventurers was not large in comparison to today's travelers, so their impact was not as obvious or severe as it is today in America. Therein lies the real problem (please don't try to use statistics to PROVE BEYOND A DOUBT THAT THE STATISTICAL NORM IN IMMIGRATION IN 1850 WAS PROPORTIONATELY MORE SEVERE THAN IN 2006). We are talking about an entirely different world than the 1700's, 1800's, 1900's or even up until the 1940's. In those times there was not the active mobility as there is today nor the rapid dissemination of information or the worldwide terror threat, and if that was not enough, we have absorbed over 12 Million ILLEGAL IMMIGRANTS into our country and they are taxing our ability to adapt.

About now all the bleeding hearts are rising up on their haunches, honing their canned rhetoric, raising their voices to a soprano falsetto (do you notice that these illegal alien protector's (IAP's) voices tip the top of the shriek scale), and are screaming at the top of their voices, "these poor souls are doing jobs we Americans are unwilling to do." THINK. If they are doing jobs we are unwilling to do, WHAT WAS HAPPENING TO THOSE JOBS BEFORE THE WILLING WORKER ILLEGAL ALIENS SHOWED UP INSIDE OUR BORDERS?????????

Now, let's go to another example to answer the statements of the liberal left that we are discriminating against Mexicans and especially illegal aliens. First of all, I thought these self same liberals had told us that these people were LATINOS not Mexicans...why the change? Next, they say we are HATERS. What a good word in order to further inflame a very emotional issue. Get that adrenaline flowing! I'm going to give you a real life example: I work with a Mexican who also happens to be an American (I absolutely detest the various terms: African American, Mexican American, and others) because his family legally immigrated to the US in the 1950's. They assimilated into the American way of life, followed the American dream, learned the American language and made their children do the same. This co-worker is extremely confrontational when it comes to the illegal immigration situation. He feels there is ABSOLUTELY NOTHING WRONG WITH 15 TO 20 MILLION INTRUDERS ENTERING AMERICA. Yes, I said intruders which is a more descriptive term for their status (intrude: to come in without permission or welcome) than illegal alien. This definition is on target! Further, this guy believes this massive intrusion is a good thing and is so closed minded that he almost goes to battle stations when anyone expresses contrary points of view. To further compromise the situation, he likes to introduce "the race card." I got very tired of listening to this person attempting to run over everyone so I decided to confront him intelligently with an analogous predicament.

I asked him (in front of a number of people because I didn't want him to possibly go off on me) if he would truthfully give me an answer to a question and he answered that he would. So I offered the following: He, his wife, and his three children were living quietly in their five bedroom home, experiencing life in a "normal" manner. He went to work, his wife cleaned and cooked and did the family shopping, the kids attended school, and their daily lives were fairly repetitious but they were, for the most part, very happy. Then two people from The Sudan showed up one day, entered the home without permission, and began to set up their life in their new surroundings. They helped clean the house, mowed the grass, cleaned the windows, trimmed the bushes and trees, washed the clothes, washed the family cars, cleaned the chimney, and took out the garbage...all the jobs the family was not happy doing. The new family members ate the same food, so the family had to portion the food for seven rather than five. The new family members also expected their medical costs would be assumed by the original family as well as setting aside sufficient funds for college. Now I turned to him and asked, what he thought of the situation. And predictably, He became very irate, called me a hater and a racist. I turned to him and said very quietly but emphatically...this is precisely the social situation that all we Americans find our selves in with the illegal aliens from Mexico. He then walked away and we have not spoken again on any subject for over a month...I hope I made some inroad into his myopia.

One of his more eloquent arguments is that we are impinging on the illegal's civil rights. Civil rights of which country? Correct me if I am wrong, but a person falls under the umbrella of civil rights in a country when he is protected by those rights through CITIZENSHIP...Right? For instance, if I travel to Turkey and open a newspaper and publish news that is biased against the government, or I decide to hold protests against the government, what are my civil rights?? NONE! I would be incarcerated with only a perfunctory trial, thrown in a jail where we in America would not put a mad pit bull dog, never to see the light of day again...Midnight Express mean anything to you? Civil rights DO NOT ACCRUE TO VISITORS whether they are in this country legally or illegally. Only citizens of that particular country are afforded the protections of civil rights in that country. Personally, I do not understand why some American citizens believe that anyone who IS NOT a citizen of this country should have any rights, much less superior rights to those who have come before and followed required immigration requirements. And that's all I've got to say about that!

NEWS FLASH!!! Today, February 13, 2007, we have reached a new low in the quest of the almighty dollar. Bank of America has inaugurated a new credit card program to assist the Illegal Intruders (and also potential terrorists) at the expense of all the rest of us because they do not have to follow established credit requirement restrictions. To entice these non-citizens to "enter our economic system and make them feel welcome," when applying for credit they WILL NOT BE REQUIRED TO HAVE A VALID SOCIAL SECURITY CARD. Doesn't that chap your ass? For the sake of greed, this bank (Bank of Un-America) is taking us one small step toward the slippery slope. Remember "inch by inch"?   DO NO LET THIS HAPPEN—-NOW IS THE TIME TO DRAW THE LINE, TAKE A STAND, AND DIG YOUR TOES IN THE SAND!!! It is up to you and you and you. Please, if you love this land of the free and home of the brave, get up off your complacent rear end and cancel all your B of A accounts...VOTE with your MONEY. I promise, if enough of you do react, the bank will retract this stupid promotion TODAY. THINK!!

The very disturbing part of this issue is the FACT that the Mexican government not only condones this exodus from its own country, but actively encourages it by providing precise maps to follow when leaving Mexico and crossing into the US. There actually is a packet that contains food and water and maps showing the safest routes and what to do once they have entered America AND all these materials are provided by the Mexican government! Now ask yourself, why would this government encourage its own populace to leave the country of their birth. Duh! Their objectives are all related to the money issue. Again, IT"S NOT THE MONEY, but after you shovel through all the horse manure what you find at the bottom is MONEY. First of all, these illegal and even legal aliens send Billions of Dollars via wire to Mexico every year. This cash flow into Mexico is second only as a source of revenue to Mexico's nationalized petroleum revenues. Secondly, they are shipping (yes shipping, because they actively encourage these people's northward trek) millions of their brothers and sisters to the US to reduce the crippling costs that were bankrupting their own economic system. After all, big brother Uncle Sam will take care of their food, shelter, and medical needs and the illegals will wire transfer mucho dinero to the coffers of Mexico...at a rate of $20 billion per year that adds up in a hurry. A billion here, a billion there and pretty soon you have enough to super size your burger order. Sounds like the politically correct and Christian things to do, right? ABSOLUTELY NOT! This atrocity is neither Christian nor politically correct. The only words to describe these actions are stupid, inane, politically incorrect, and just ANTI-AMERICAN! There, I've said it...now I'm in deep do-do with the Kennedy and Soros types. Well it is about time WE THE PEOPLE BECAME WE THE PEOPLE WHO AREN'T AFRAID TO STAND UP AND SAY ENOUGH! Do not be afraid; they can't eat you and remember what Franklin Delano Roosevelt said in one of his more famous speeches, "the only thing you have to fear is fear itself." THINK!!!!!

No matter what any of you say, you know deep in your hearts that I am right, even if your public words say I am wrong. You have been "inched by inched" until you don't have an uncorrupted thought in your head. You think you believe that those poor souls who have entered our country from Mexico should be welcomed with open arms, given jobs, given credit cards without required identity papers, allowed to attend our public schools gratis, provided free medical care, given citizenship to their babies that are born on American soil, given low cost housing...the next thing will be to allow one of them to become President of The United States of America (which soon, if the liberals have their way, will include all of Central America and some offshore islands as well). This political correctness (who the hell ever came up with that term?) is not correct. It is a way of using our Christian goodness and fairness to make us so sorry for a particular group or situation that we fold like a five-dollar suitcase. Well guys, the smorgasbord is over because WE THE PEOPLE are sick and tired of you telling us what is politically correct and what is not; what is best for us and what is not; what is the Christian thing to do and what is not; why teachers are not allowed to discipline unruly children in their classes; why we can not have a Holy Bible in front of a government building, when we are one nation UNDER GOD; why we can not place a Christmas tree in a mall; why our children can not say prayers in school; why American citizens from Mexico are called Mexican Americans rather than Americans; why there are African Americans rather than Americans (why is it proper to be African American when it is fairly evident that these fine citizens are black and probably have African ancestry). These descriptive adjectives identifying someone's ethnic/racial background is, to me, repugnant, extremely racial, and calculatedly divisive. It is, I believe, another insidious way to further separate and weaken the moral fiber of all our great citizens. Please, all citizens regardless of your genetic beginnings, let us come together, despite our inevitable differences, as ONE AMERICAN and throw the scoundrels out. WE THE PEOPLE...THINK!!!!!!!!

What does all this have to do with illegal immigration?— Nothing and everything. I am trying to stimulate your gray matter that has been marinated in the ceaseless cauldron of political correctness. I, for one, do not want to be political and I sure do not want to be correct—-I only want to be fair and equal to every citizen of America—- ONLY THIS AND NOTHING MORE.

Let's get busy and put us back on the right track (the one not espoused by Ted and George S.) Even my hero, George W. Bush, is (I believe) wavering and vacillating on the Illegal immigration issue. No one has ever said I was shy, so here goes...First of all we MUST SECURE OUR BORDERS AT ALL COSTS. We all (Republicans, Democrats, or whatever your political leanings are), MUST put aside our petty bickering and political posturing and make this PRIORITY ONE. I don't care if it is a physical fence or electronic wizardry or increasing the Border Patrol and giving them absolute power to secure our borders at all cost! Preventative medicine is always the preferred medicine and the least costly. This goes for the illegal immigration issue as well. Once the borders are secure, all efforts must be undertaken to extradite the illegal people who are in our prisons...the estimate is that approximately 30% of the current prison population is illegal aliens. When we get rid of these criminals, it will not only free our society of the burden of housing, feeding, and providing medical treatment for these scum, but also reduce the overcrowded prison situation. Pretty good, two birds with one stone. Enough stones and we'll have that fence built before you know it.

Secondly, we must assimilate the remaining intruders into our society. Yes, even though they clearly broke the laws of the United States, they are here. It would be prohibitively expensive to go through the laborious extradition process, AND if we have done our job of expatriating the criminal element, the remainder has a high probability of assimilating into our society properly. Next, we have to actively secure them jobs at a fair wage, put them through the required citizenship program and when they have completed the program and have passed the required test...they will be sworn in as CITZENS OF THE UNITED STATES OF AMERICA. What a happy and proud day for them and their families and what a happy day for us because we have new citizens who will bring a new sense of excitement and energy to America...a shot in the arm for a country that has become lethargic and apathetic. COME ON NEW AMERICANS WHO HAPPEN TO BE FROM MEXICO...help us ALL move forward TOGETHER, arm in arm toward a brave new world.

THINK...THINK...THINK—WHAT A BEAUTIFUL WORLD WE CAN CREATE WITH GOD"S BLESSING IF WE WORK TOGETHER. THINK! THINK!

WAR

First of all, let's get on the same page with a general definition of war. War is an armed conflict between two nations. You can give it other definitions or use other analogies or nuances but that is a good basic description of war.

Conflict has been around since man set foot on this planet. God gave humans freedom of thought and expression and choice. As I said earlier, the uncertainty this created gave God a degree of excitement to His here-to-fore predictable existence. God did foresee this conflict and knew it would lead to hostility, but at least He would be able to observe what His creations were capable of without direct Divine intervention.

Hostility can express itself in an almost infinite number of alternatives from two people attacking each other all the way to nations waging war against each other. This type of activity began when we set foot on the planet and continues today.

The more technologically advanced we have become, the more vicious and catastrophic have been the results of the conflicts to the point that in the late 1940's someone came up with the brilliant idea of making war civilized. BRILLIANT?........NO!....STUPID, INFINTILE AND UNBELIEVABLY NAIVE...YES!!!!

No matter what I say from this point forward in this chapter, there will be those who say I am a war monger, insensitive, barbaric, cruel, inhumane, and so on. Well, in a way they are right, BUT in a very real (NO SPIN, NO POLITICALLY CORRECT, NO POLLYANNA MYOPIC EUPHORIA) sense they are absolutely wrong. I will say that war is war and if nations have reached the point of no return...and yes there are times that further diplomacy is futile, then war becomes inevitable. It is a great deal like, if a bully on the school yard has continued to focus his attention on a "perceived " weaker person, and this action has gone on for a long period and has actually escalated to a point of critical mass...then something is going to happen.

Seldom do wars or even battles begin "at the drop of a hat." More often, these conflicts have been brewing for very long periods and have their genesis in some long forgotten incident that in retrospect is inane. But be that as it may, once a conflict of this magnitude has begun, rules of conduct or even general understandings are a dichotomy of purpose. These ideas of war and civilized action are MUTUALLY EXCLUSIVE. Therefore, attempts to make war more humane are not only intellectually senseless but they are an infantile attempt to make something that is entirely non civilized into something that has a single premise...that being the destruction or humiliation or total elimination of one's enemy. People (usually those who have NEVER been slapped, hit or kicked) say we must protect our humanity with attempts such as The Geneva Conventions that began after World War II in 1949.

We view these "progressive programs" as glorious steps toward a more civilized, Christian set of codes of conduct for war. Well, "dear hearts" all this sounds good to your kinder, gentler nature but it DON'T PLAY ON THE WORLD'S STAGE!!! THINK!!! It is like telling Mike Tyson to go into the ring, not to knock the stuffing out of his opponent and destroy him, but to out petty pat him into gentle submission...WRONG!!!!

Even on this smaller scale, you have to admit it makes absolutely no sense. The whole idea of war is to win at all costs! Rationalize all you want, but this is the true nature of and objective of war. You need to stop wringing your hands and shaking your heads and just realize the truth of what I am saying. However, if this is true, what can be done to stop this carnage and forever eliminate it from the face of the earth and thereby make all we humans more godly in our thoughts, words, and deeds?

I actually hate to tell you this, but I must! That glorious day will not come until Judgment Day. Sure we can try and put salve on our emotional and religious wounds of guilt, but the truth of the matter is that war is war and all attempts to "make it better" are like blowing into the trade winds at Pali Point in Hawaii. Our only hope is that our redeeming Savior will Return In Glory and cleanse us of all our sins no matter our religious beliefs...even the atheists, who you recall have a religion...a religion of non belief. I'll bet the farm that these atheists will fall on their irreverent knees about two times faster than the rest of us when that day comes. Until that day, try to love your neighbor, but if he is non responsive or belligerent...let the conflict (war) begin. And that's all I've got to say about that. THINK!! THINK WITH YOUR BRAIN, NOT YOUR HEART!!! BUT THINK!!!!

Another attempt at "civilizing" the war process was the brilliant idea of placing news reporters in the general vicinity of the armed conflict. The espoused rationale for this innovation was that it would bring the war home to Americans in an up close and personal manner. This innovation came from the very highest echelons of dogmatic, leftist, liberal media moguls such as Arthur Sulzberger, Jr., the man in charge of The Old York Times. Mr. Sulzberger doesn't even attempt to hide his extreme leftist liberal bent; in fact, he is proud of his bias in reporting "all the news that is fit to slant."

However, the leftist liberal media (including TV and radio and other printed media) hit a new low in creative journalism with this new idea and even came up with a trendy, with-it name for these fast track reporters...imbedded journalists. All this sounds very creative, cutting edge, and a fairly daring way of bringing the war home to the average citizen. That is the spin Mr. Sulzberger and "the boys" are attempting to sell to all of us back home. THINK!!!!!

Number one, none of these reporters are truly at the front. They are in the vicinity but only occasionally might they run into danger (my sympathies to Bob Woodward and his family and condolences to Daniel Pearl and his family). However, this war is much different than a World War II, I, or even the Korean War. It is very similar to the Vietnam War where the idea of imbedded reporters had its genesis.

You might agree or disagree with what I'm about to write, but keep an open mind and try to appreciate my logic. Let's go back to World War II and put imbedded reporters in England a month or so before D-Day. The reporters are hungry for a story and learn about a major offensive that will focus on a massive assault on Normandy Beach. If those reporters operated in today's freedom of speech environment the headlines of The New York Times would have read...ALLIES GO FOR BROKE ON NORMANDY. Just imagine where you and your family would be living today and what your lives would be like under the rule of The Third Reich. That headline would have been printed under the aegis of the free speech, freedom of the press idiots, none of whom have spent one single day in a foxhole. How does that make you feel? Does freedom of speech and freedom of the press allow these executive suite warriors (how's the bagel with lox and cream cheese) the absolute right to not only place even one soldier in harm's way but to also place the entire historical imperative in danger? THINK!!!

That is exactly what these mindless nincompoops think is good journalism...and if you disagree or don't like it...we'll call the American Criminal Liberties Union pit bulls out to rip you to shreds. Get a life. You guys are just a slovenly bunch of overpaid newspaper writers who think they run the world. WRONG! You are a danger because you don't understand your function. You are not the President of the United States. You are not a Senator, Representative, Governor, Mayor, City Council member, or even a dogcatcher. You have been led by people like Mr. Sulzberger to believe that you are a mover of mountains, a molder of opinions...WRONG! In your heart of hearts you realize you are just a newspaper reporter and your job (nothing wrong with it, it's a noble profession) is to report what has already happened. Well, I guess there goes any chance of my book making the Best Seller's List in The New York Times!

Sure inquiring minds want to know...at least that's what

the MT's have told us, but we do not need to know how a war is progressing one nanosecond at a time. Do not put your inflated estimation of your own self-worth and your insatiable need for perceived importance and power ahead of the Prime Directive. If you have lost sight of the Prime Directive of war (it is not to win friends or win a popularity poll), it is to win and to win at all costs while at the same time incurring as few casualties as possible.

CHANGE

All we hear about right now is change. We need change. We deserve change. Change is good. Change is necessary. Change will get us out of all our problems. Change, Change, Change. But what do you get when you achieve a change and what will this change bode?

Change for change's sake achieves nothing more than a degree of difference in a situation. The question is, does this change warrant the inevitable upheaval? Remember one of the famous laws of physics...for every action, there is an equal and opposite reaction. This even holds true in human situations such as love, marriage, hate, envy, fear, happiness, and others. It also applies to political, social, legal, and religious circumstances, as well as local, national, and even international situations.

Let's first explore change in a situation near and dear to all of us...the institution of marriage. Two people come together for various obvious and inexplicable reasons. They pledge their undying love for each other in front of their friends and families and the officiating person declares them to be married and not till death do they part. Occasionally, and in today's world more than occasionally, these soul mates drift apart and develop real or imaginary differences that cause them to seek a way out of their union. To these people I say, unless there is a definitive reason (abuse-—physical or mental, drug addiction, alcoholism, insanity, and so on....you get the picture, right?) to seek a divorce you should exhaust all avenues available before throwing the bum or bumette out, especially if it is for a new potential bum or bumette). The reason I say this is because all you are doing is trading one known quantity for another unknown quantity.

Of course, the new Mr. or Ms. Right is wonderful and is exactly the perfect person you have been looking for your entire life—your soul mate, but I ask you...isn't that exactly how you felt about your current mate when your endorphins were raging through your veins just a few years ago? THINK!!!! Don't let your friends (probably single or envious of your marriage) or the local friendly divorce attorney (you know, the guy who needs to make a payment or two on his new Mercedes) sway you into an ill-conceived or precipitous action. THINK!!

Now let's go to another timely situation...the 2006-2007 U. S. House and Senatorial elections. All you could hear was "WE WANT CHANGE, WE NEED CHANGE, THE AMERICAN PEOPLE DESERVE CHANGE , CHANGE, CHANGE, CHANGE. Change is a very powerful idea, it can improve your life or destroy it, it can unseat rulers and Presidents, and it can even make an automobile continue on its trip after having a flat tire. After years of fighting in Iraq and years of the obviously biased left wing media showing one IED explosion after another and telling the American citizens that we were surely losing the war, the American voters had but one thing to do...vote out the Senators and Representatives who had sided with President Bush and caused this catastrophe. Day after day pounding and pounding away at the "fact" that we were losing the war won over sufficient numbers of voters to effect CHANGE. But may I ask, a change to what? THINK!!!

The Democratic majority in both houses of Congress will do what? What is their plan? We failed to get definitive answers to that question before we went to the polls like programmed lambs to the slaughter following the JUDAS GOAT of WE (who exactly is we?...if Bill can be confused about "is", I can be confused about we. That we surely did not included me!). What change, Nancy? I hear NOTHING CONSTRUCTIVE! All I hear out of you and the boys from Massachusetts, New York, Pennsylvania, California, and other states is bring the boys home. Don't get me wrong, I too want all our brave young soldiers home safe and sound, BUT at what cost to the security of the United States and the rest of the world in the next decade?

Remember what Al Queda has accomplished in only 20 years. With a victory base in Iraq, I shudder to extrapolate the growth of the malignant Islamic Jihadists. At what cost has the United States played its hand of CHANGE!!!! THINK!!!!!!!!

I could go on and on with one example after another, but you are smart people and by now you have the idea. All I wanted to achieve in writing this book (because, it's not about the money) was to get you intelligent, wonderful, articulate people to throw off the shackles of the MT's, ET's, ST's, TB's, and IAP's and all the other devils who would attempt to rob you of your God given abilities to think for yourself.

My prayers are with all of you. If I have helped even a little bitty bit (West Texas slang for a small amount), please let me know so I may share in your success.

ONE WORLD ECONOMY

One World Economy? Sounds intriguing. Sounds progressive.
Sounds hopeful. Sounds like the future. Sounds necessary.
Sounds like the right (Christian) thing to do. WRONG!!!

Has anyone ever heard about economics? If we are all
part of one big economy, where is the competition that creates
"BETTER, FASTER, CHEAPER"? Correct me if I am wrong,
but the entire reason that there is progress and an improving
economic environment that fosters an ever-improving lifestyle
is that nasty word COMPETITION...right?

If we move forward "into the gathering twilight" of a one
world economy, the light at the end of the tunnel will be an
eighteen thousand ton locomotive that will result in DOOM to
the world as we know it. Sure there are "Supply and Demand"
and "Economy of Scale," but whoever believes in this One
World Economy must have used crib notes to pass Economics
101. Being "with it and politically correct" is what all these
MT'S, ET's, ST's, TB's and IAP's are selling out of their snake
oil wagon. It is good for all of us! It is inevitable! It is the savior
of mankind! It is the wave of the future!

For one, it was my understanding that Jesus was the savior
of mankind (Muhammad if you are Islamic, as well as others,
depending on your religion). And when it comes to waves, does
the word tsunami conjure up visions of prosperity? One of the
things I know is that people are all different, be it good or be
it bad, which is a fact of life. That is what God wanted and no
amount of tinkering from you "globalists"will make that fact
any more palatable or acceptable or have ANY chance to work.

There, I've said it, and I'm glad I did and I used a reference to The Deity.

The main arguments used by these secular economists (those guys who cheated their way through Economics 101 or made less than B's) are: globalization is inevitable; it will better serve the economic and material needs of all humans in an equal manner; it will eliminate worldwide poverty by distributing wealth more equitably; and it will cause an improvement in the ecology because there will be a uniform global ecological mandate.

First, there is nothing inevitable except death and taxes (unless this globalization can eradicate this nuisance)...Maybe it has some merit after all! To hear these theorists spin their stories is truly mind boggling, BUT remember "inch by inch" and "a lie told a thousand times." And if I might digress into an earlier chapter, these so called experts are the moles that buried themselves into our education, media, legal, religious, and political systems in the late 1960's, 1970's and 1980's. These moles have dug their burrows deep and well and are now in seats of influence and power and they are spewing forth all their seeds of progressive change. Their numbers are legion and many of their positions are very respected so do not be fooled or overwhelmed by who they are or what they proclaim to be the truth. THINK!!!!

Second, globalization will not better serve anyone's needs except for those like, for instance Mr. Soros, opportunists who will fill their pockets without a second thought for the betterment of man. These people slap your back with one hand and pick your pocket with the other...all the while looking you in the eyes and smiling. Remember, Money Trumps Everything Else! This is a truism in all things whether you are talking about business, politics, education, or even religion because those with the money usually get their way. Remember the economic "Golden Rule"...those who have the gold, rule. It is really that simple. You can protest, argue, deny, or even hold your breathe and stomp your feet, but unless you have the money...you lose! I hate to be so jaded but you know I am correct and their agendas are far different than yours or mine. Not that wealth is bad, especially if you came about your wealth by honest hard working toil, but most extremely wealthy people are only focused on one thing...making more money and extending their power and influence over the rest of us.

Third, their position that their plans would eliminate worldwide poverty by distributing wealth more equitably is less than nonsensical. If it weren't such a serious problem and a problem that is hurtful to true religious humanitarians, I would fall down and have a good belly laugh at the crap these moles are trying to spoon feed us without even one teaspoon of sugar. Hey guys, you must have ingested so much of your tripe that you cannot distinguish truth from near truth or outright lies. All you do is find a subject, and test what the potential intensity level might be if presented with the appropriate "spin." As a prime example, we can turn on the television or radio any hour of the day or night and hear...GLOBAL WARMING!!! THE END IS NEAR!!!...If we don't do something TODAY all the polar bears will die and every coastal city around the world will be flooded. These denizens of gloom and doom (unless THEY are allowed to lead us out of this morass) are led by Mr. Sincerity himself...the late great last Vice President of The United States of America...Mr. Al Gore. To his credit, Mr. Gore has espoused this crusade for over fifteen years so he is no Johnny-come-lately. Al has positioned himself to benefit financially and politically and is running a much better and more successful campaign for this cause than he was able to for his own Presidential election attempt.

Sure there are many hypothetical excuses for global warming and a few very real reasons and the reasons need to be addressed and corrected over time. By over time, I do not mean 100 years, even though whatever global warming exists has been cumulative over a few centuries. The emissions from internal combustion engines, coal-fired systems, and reckless burning of various human created wastes are things that we can effectively reduce if we allow the private sector to attack the problems. KEEP THE GOVERNMENT OUT OF THE

REMEDY...government, like my late father said, "is able to screw up a steel ball with a rubber hammer."

Every day we see the graphic films of the poor polar bear swimming from one melting ice flow to another and then your mind is allowed to conjure up the pitiful death of the bear as it swims until it can swim no more. The ONLY PROBLEM with this "emotional documentary" is that it is fictitious. The truth is that there are at least six (6) times as many polar bears today as existed in 1975. Yes, the polar bear is no where near anyone's near extinction list...even The Old York Times can't put enough of their highly paid spinners on this situation and make it a world shattering problem.

We also see endless footage of glaciers melting and ice shelves separating from the mass and cascading into the ocean with a mighty splash. This, the alarmists tell you is proof positive that The End Is Near and it is all caused by GLOBAL WARMING. Again, wrong! The average worldwide temperature (whatever that means and by whomever it is measured) has risen...yes it has risen a gargantuan amount of 0.7 degrees Fahrenheit (sorry for using that word Mr. Moore) over the last two hundred years. That is as far back as average worldwide temperatures have been measured consistently. I hate to tell you doomsayers, but in the grand scheme of things 0.7 degrees is, while notable, quite an expected variation. In fact, as nearly as can be APPROXIMATED, the earth's average temperature has only fluctuated about 8.0 degrees from the last ice age some 18,000 years ago to today. AND over the last 3 billion years...YES I SAID BILLION YEARS...the earth's average temperature has only fluctuated ten degrees (between 12 degrees Celsius and 22 degrees Celsius). I dare you to identify any other phenomenon that has exhibited less variation than the earth's average annual temperature. So you can see and easily understand that there is a built in variation in the earth's temperature much the same as variation in the amount of water in a bottle of Dasani...If you don't believe me, set eight bottles side by side and view the variations for yourself. THINK!!!

Remember not everything is as portrayed and not everyone

or the words they write or the words they speak should ever be given any more or any less credence just because of who they are or what institution they represent. THINK FOR YOURSELF!!!

UNITED WE STAND, DIVIDED WE FALL

Now that you have finished the book, what are you going to do? There are many directions and avenues you can follow...and it is all up to you!

You can lay the book down and walk away and say, "That was a great book," or "That was a stupid book," or "I wish I had written the book," or "What possessed Bob to write this book," or, or, or "Let's put this book in our library," or "Let's sell the book to Half-Priced-Books," or "Throw the book out, dear; it isn't worth keeping." Your own reaction will be up to you and I genuinely do not care what your reaction is UNLESS you sit down, review what these pages have said to you and your loved ones and you make a vow to no longer allow these "terrorists in sheep's clothing" to manipulate your own thoughts. Say NO MORE and mean it. It will be a long journey that will take dedication and nerves of titanium, BUT the end is only an inch away. Do not be dissuaded, do not be discouraged...WE OUT NUMBER THESE ANARCHISTS by at least 10,000 to 1. How can I say this? Because I'm Bob and I truly believe that the vast majority of Americans believe as I do...we've just gotten temporarily complacent.

Remember you are fighting for the America that you know and love...the America that stands for equality for all...the America that allows everyone to achieve based on ability, desire and willingness to sacrifice...the America that attracts so many to its promise...the America that truly is the last great hope for civilization, BUT we must fix a lot of things before America is back on track again. We have shared a large number of the things that need fixing and the amazing thing is that they can be fixed.

Be we Democrats or Republicans, black or white or brown or yellow, tall or short, skinny or heavy, bald or hairy, weak or strong, able or disabled, rich or poor, and so on...WE ARE ALL AMERICANS. We are not African-Americans, we are not Mexican-Americans, we are not hyphenated Americans, so let's start acting like Americans. All these "terrorists" have had their way too long...throw them out with yesterday's garbage...let them wallow in familiar surroundings. They thrive on creating the illusions...illusions that we want and need ethnic separation when what we want is ethnic appreciation; illusions that we want everything to be "politically correct," when all we actually want is fairness for all and all laws to be dispensed equally for all without exception; illusions that some deserve special treatment but we want equal treatment for all in education, the law, medical availability, and education. If someone breaks the law, we want them to be sentenced according to the law—-no exceptions, no special treatment. Rules in a society are there for a reason and if someone decides to break the rule, they will be punished according to the then current law. If WE THE PEOPLE determine that a law needs revision or elimination, then WE THE PEOPLE will vote for that change. We do not need any politico, judge, or extremist in the media or position of power to tell us what is good for us. Thank God we can think for ourselves.

If we have all the above, I truly believe that the American Spirit and Drive will propel this great country and its beautiful population to greater heights than even Bob can envision. Become more active in your community. Vote in every election. Get to know your neighbors. Get a little closer to God. SMILE... it can't hurt. AND MOST IMPORTANTLY OF ALL...love yourself and your family!

It has been my pleasure to share with you some of my thoughts...THANK YOU for allowing me to become part of your thought processes. THINK!!!!!! And continue to think...be proactive rather than reactive or inactive.